CliffsNotes™

STACKS

Huxley's
Brave New World

By Dr. Charles Higgins, Ph.D., and
Dr. Regina Higgins, Ph.D

IN THIS BOOK

D0003106

- Learn about the Life and Backg

- Preview and Introduction to the Novel

- Explore themes, character development, and recurring images in the Critical Commentaries

- Examine in-depth Character Analyses

- Acquire an understanding of the novel with Critical Essays

- Reinforce what you learn with CliffsNotes Review

- Find additional information to further your study in CliffsNotes Resource Center and online at www.cliffsnotes.com

IDG
BOOKS
WORLDWIDE

About the Author

Charles and Regina Higgins have worked together as educational writers for fifteen years. They each have a Ph.D. in English from Indiana University.

Publisher's Acknowledgments

Editorial

Project Editor: Tracy Barr
Acquisitions Editor: Greg Tubach
Editorial Assistant: Michelle Hacker
Glossary Editors: The editors and staff of Webster's New World Dictionaries

Production

Indexer: York Production Services, Inc.
Proofreader: York Production Services, Inc.
IDG Books Indianapolis Production Department

CliffsNotes™ Huxley's *Brave New World*
Published by
IDG Books Worldwide, Inc.
An International Data Group Company
919 E. Hillsdale Blvd.
Suite 400
Foster City, CA 94404

www.idgbooks.com (IDG Books Worldwide Web site)

www.cliffsnotes.com (CliffsNotes Web site)

ISBN: 0-7645-8583-5

Printed in the United States of America

10 9 8 7 6 5 4 3 2 1

1V/RY/QV/QQ/IN

Distributed in the United States by IDG Books Worldwide, Inc.

Library of Congress Cataloging-in-Publication Data
Higgins, Charles.
    CliffsNotes Huxley's Brave New World / by Charles Higgins and Regina Higgins.
        p.   cm.
    ISBN 0-7645-8583-5 (alk. paper)
    1. Huxley, Aldous, 1894–1963. Brave New World--Examinations--Study guides. 2. Science fiction, English--Examinations--Study guides. Dystopias in literature.
    I. Title: Brave New World. II. Higgins, Regina Kirby.
PR6015.U9 B63 2000
823'.912--dc21   00–037020
                                             CIP

Distributed by CDG Books Canada Inc. for Canada; by Transworld Publishers Limited in the United Kingdom; by IDG Norge Books for Norway; by IDG Sweden Books for Sweden; by IDG Books Australia Publishing Corporation Pty. Ltd. for Australia and New Zealand; by Trans-Quest Publishers Pte Ltd. for Singapore, Malaysia, Thailand, Indonesia, and Hong Kong; by Gotop Information Inc. for Taiwan; by ICG Muse, Inc. for Japan; by Intersoft for South Africa; by Eyrolles for France; by International Thomson Publishing for Germany, Austria and Switzerland; by Distribuidora Cuspide for Argentina; by LR International for Brazil; by Galileo Libros for Chile; by Ediciones ZETA S.C.R. Ltda. for Peru; by WS Computer Publishing Corporation, Inc., for the Philippines; by Contemporanea de Ediciones for Venezuela; by Express Computer Distributors for the Caribbean and West Indies; by Micronesia Media Distributor, Inc. for Micronesia; by Chips Computadoras S.A. de C.V. for Mexico; by Editorial Norma de Panama S.A. for Panama; by American Bookshops for Finland.

For general information on IDG Books Worldwide's books in the U.S., please call our Consumer Customer Service department at **800-762-2974**. For reseller information, including discounts and premium sales, please call our Reseller Customer Service department at **800-434-3422**.

For information on where to purchase IDG Books Worldwide's books outside the U.S., please contact our International Sales department at **317-596-5530** or fax **317-572-4002**.

For consumer information on foreign language translations, please contact our Customer Service department at **1-800-434-3422**, fax 317-572-4002, or e-mail rights@idgbooks.com.

For information on licensing foreign or domestic rights, please phone **+1-650-653-7098**.

For sales inquiries and special prices for bulk quantities, please contact our Order Services department at **800-434-3422** or write to the address above.

For information on using IDG Books Worldwide's books in the classroom or for ordering examination copies, please contact our Educational Sales department at **800-434-2086** or fax **317-572-4005**.

For press review copies, author interviews, or other publicity information, please contact our Public Relations department at **650-653-7000** or fax **650-653-7500**.

For authorization to photocopy items for corporate, personal, or educational use, please contact Copyright Clearance Center, 222 Rosewood Drive, Danvers, MA 01923, or fax **978-750-4470**.

Table of Contents

How to Use This Book

CliffsNotes Huxley's *Brave New World* supplements the original work, giving you background information about the author, an introduction to the novel, a graphical character map, critical commentaries, expanded glossaries, and a comprehensive index. CliffsNotes Review tests your comprehension of the original text and reinforces learning with questions and answers, practice projects, and more. For further information on Aldous Huxley, *Brave New World*, and *Brave New World Revisited*, check out the CliffsNotes Resource Center.

CliffsNotes provides the following icons to highlight essential elements of particular interest:

Reveals the underlying themes in the work.

Helps you to more easily relate to or discover the depth of a character.

Uncovers elements such as setting, atmosphere, mystery, passion, violence, irony, symbolism, tragedy, foreshadowing, and satire.

Enables you to appreciate the nuances of words and phrases.

Don't Miss Our Web Site

Discover classic literature as well as modern-day treasures by visiting the Cliffs-Notes Web site at www.cliffsnotes.com. You can obtain a quick download of a CliffsNotes title, purchase a title in print form, browse our catalog, or view online samples.

You'll also find interactive tools that are fun and informative, links to interesting Web sites, tips, articles, and additional resources to help you, not only for literature, but for test prep, finance, careers, computers, and the Internet too. See you at www.cliffs notes.com!

LIFE AND BACKGROUND OF THE AUTHOR

Early Years

Aldous Huxley was born July 26, 1894, in the village of Godalming, Surrey, England. The third son of Leonard Huxley, a writer, editor, and teacher, and Julia Arnold, also a teacher, the young Aldous grew up in a family of well-connected, well-known writers, scientists, and educators.

At Aldous' birth, the Huxley family and their relatives already commanded literary and philosophical attention in Victorian England. Huxley's grandfather, biologist T. H. Huxley, gained recognition in the nineteenth century as the writer who introduced Charles Darwin's theory of evolution to a wide public and coined the word "agnostic." The elder Huxley's writing contributed to the growing debate on science and religion, a theme that would capture the imagination of his grandson, Aldous.

Huxley's mother was a niece of poet and essayist Matthew Arnold, who expressed the moral struggles of the modern age and the retreat of a religion-based culture. Matthew's father, Thomas Arnold, head of Rugby School, had presided with earnest devotion over the theory and practice of education in his time. Thus Aldous grew up in an atmosphere in which thought on science, religion, and education informed and even dominated family life.

Living up to the expectations of "Grandpater," as T. H. Huxley was known in his family, constituted a full-time, exhausting job for the children—Aldous included. Academic and professional brilliance was expected as a matter of course, with no excuses allowed. A family tendency toward depression compounded by this pressure may have contributed to the suicide of Trevenan, Aldous' elder brother.

At sixteen, the sudden onset of *keratitis punctate*, an eye disease, left Aldous nearly blind and almost ruined his own chances for success. Fortunately, surgery corrected some of his vision, but Huxley would suffer from complications in vision for the rest of his life.

Education

Like all the sons of his family, Huxley attended Eton, a prestigious preparatory school, and Balliol College, Oxford. His education, then, represented a privileged road to power for wealthy and well-born British men who sometimes displayed real brilliance. Huxley was among the best of them, certainly. Poor sight caused by the eye disease prevented his pursuit of his first career choice, medicine, but he threw himself into study of literature, reading with the help of a magnifying glass. In 1915, Huxley took a First (highest honors) in English Literature.

A less formal, but nonetheless important part of Huxley's education was his regular attendance at Lady Ottoline Morrell's get-togethers, which provided many literary, artistic, and political reformers and experimenters the chance to meet and talk. Here Huxley met novelist Virginia Woolf, economist John Maynard Keynes, and critics Bertrand Russell and Clive Bell—some of the most important writers and thinkers of the time. Huxley's early exposure to the ideas of such a diverse and progressive group deeply influenced his world-view and his writing.

Jobs

After taking his degree at Oxford, Huxley returned to Eton to teach. Among his pupils was Eric Blair, who would later write such classics as *1984* and *Animal Farm* under the pseudonym "George Orwell."

From 1919 to 1921, Huxley worked as an editor on the London journal *Athenaeum*, one of the best-known publications of the time. Huxley also contributed to *Vanity Fair* and *Vogue* before devoting himself entirely to his own fiction and essay writing in 1924.

Literary Writing

Huxley's first published work was a collection of his poetry, *The Burning Wheel* (1916), written when he was still in his early twenties. French novelist Marcel Proust praised Huxley's early efforts, and Huxley seemed destined for life as a poet. But with the publication of his first two novels, *Crome Yellow* (1921) and *Antic Hay* (1923), Huxley emerged as a particularly witty chronicler of modern life among the educated and pretentious.

Huxley further solidified his reputation as a satirist with the novel *Point Counter Point* (1928), a scathing study of the breakdown of commonly held social values. Huxley followed up with another satire, which would prove to be his most popular work—*Brave New World* (1932).

Like his previous novels, *Brave New World* is a "novel of ideas," in which the themes the author wishes to explore take center stage, determining the action as well as the characterization. *Brave New World* continued in Huxley's familiar irreverent fictional style, showing readers the absurdity of strongly held but little examined beliefs.

The work also marked a change in Huxley himself. The setting of *Brave New World*—a future London rather than the familiar country houses and town houses of his previous fiction—seems to have broken Huxley out of some habits of mind. In *Brave New World*, Huxley takes the problem of evil much more seriously than in the past. The satirist had begun to evolve into the social philosopher.

After the publication of *Brave New World*, Huxley left England, living with his wife, Maria, first in New Mexico—the site of the Savage Reservation in *Brave New World*—and later in California, where surgery restored much of his vision.

In his new home, Huxley became involved in the study and practice of mysticism. His new philosophical outlook informed his novel *Eyeless in Gaza* (1936), which promoted pacifism on the eve of World War II. *After Many a Summer Dies the Swan* (1939) makes the case for the emptiness of materialism. Gradually, Huxley moved toward mystical writings, far from the tone of his early satire. *The Perennial Philosophy* (1945) and *The Doors of Perception* (1954) represent Huxley's non-fictional expression of his interests, including even experimentation with psychedelic drugs.

In Los Angeles, Huxley wrote screenplays for film versions of fictional classics such as *Jane Eyre*, *Pride and Prejudice*, and *Alice in Wonderland*. He also continued writing fiction, notably *Ape and Essence* (1948), a futuristic fiction set in Los Angeles after a nuclear war. With *Grey Eminence* (1941) and *The Devils of Loudon* (1952), Huxley looked backward to historical events to examine what he believed to be the hypocrisy of organized religion. In addition to his fiction and screenplays, the planning and writing of biographies, essays, and other works of non-fiction occupied him constantly during these years.

Huxley's last novel, *Island* (1962), returns to the theme of the future he once explored so memorably in *Brave New World*. The later novel, in which Huxley tried to create a positive vision of the future, failed to come up to readers' expectations. *Brave New World Revisited*, a series of essays addressing the themes of his early novel, represents a more successful rethinking of future (and present) social challenges.

Huxley died of cancer in California on November 22, 1963. Although his novels—especially *Brave New World*—still enjoyed great popularity, Huxley's death received little notice in the media at the time. The nation's shock over the assassination of President John F. Kennedy overshadowed news of the writer's death.

Honors and Awards

Huxley won the James Tait Black Memorial Prize for Fiction from the University of Edinburgh in 1939 for his novel *After Many a Summer Dies the Swan*. In 1959, he received the Award of Merit and Gold Medal from the American Academy and Institute of Arts and Letters and accepted an honorary Doctor of Letters degree from the University of California. The year before his death, he received the Companion of Literature from the British Royal Society of Literature.

INTRODUCTION TO THE NOVEL

Introduction

Huxley wrote *Brave New World* "between the wars"—after the upheaval of the First World War and before World War II. British society was officially at peace, but the social effects of the Great War, as it was then called, were becoming apparent. Huxley and his contemporaries wrote about changes in national feeling, questioning of long-held social and moral assumptions, and the move toward more equality among the classes and between the sexes.

Historical Background

The Russian Revolution and challenges to the British Empire abroad raised the possibility of change on a world scale. At home, the expansion of transportation and communication—the cars, telephones, and radios made affordable through mass production—also brought revolutionary changes to daily life. With the new technology, distances grew suddenly shorter and true privacy rarer. While people in industrialized societies welcomed these advances, they also worried about losing a familiar way of life, and perhaps even themselves, in the process. The nightmare vision of the fast-paced but meaningless routine of *Brave New World* reflects this widespread concern about the world of the 1920s and 1930s.

The period also brought a new questioning of traditional morality, especially regarding sex. Dress, language, and especially fiction expressed a greater openness for both women and men in their sexual lives. Some hailed this change as the beginning of true individual freedom, while others condemned it as the end of civilization itself. Huxley, with typical wit, uses the issue for irony, creating an image of the young Lenina being scolded for her lack of promiscuity. Sexual rules may change, Huxley tells his readers, but the power of convention remains the same.

Although set in the future, then, Huxley's *Brave New World* is truly a novel of its time. At a period of great change, Huxley creates a world in which all the present worrying trends have produced terrible consequences. Movement toward socialism in the 1920s, for example, becomes, in Huxley's future, the totalitarian World State. Questioning of religious beliefs and the growth of materialism, likewise, transforms into a religion of consumerism with Henry Ford as its god. And if Model T's roll off the assembly line in the present, in a stream of identical cars, then in the future, human beings will be mass-produced, too.

Huxley's future vision, by turns witty and disturbing, imagines the end of a familiar, traditional life and the triumph of all that is new and strange in the modern world.

Utopian Fiction

In constructing an imaginary world, Huxley contributes to a long tradition—the utopian fiction. "Utopia," from the Greek words for "no place" and "good place," first came into English in Sir Thomas More's work *Utopia* (1516), a fictional account of a far away nation whose characteristics invite comparison with More's England. More used his fictional Utopia to point out the problems present in his own society. Since then, writers have created utopias to challenge readers to think about the underlying assumptions of their own culture. *Gulliver's Travels* (1726), by Jonathan Swift, seems at first to be a book of outlandish travel stories. Yet throughout the narratives, Swift employs his fictional worlds ironically to make serious arguments about the injustices of his own Britain. In utopian fiction, imagination becomes a way to explore alternatives in political, social, and religious life.

In Huxley's time, the most popular writer of utopian fiction was H.G. Wells, author of *The Time Machine* (1895), *The War of the Worlds* (1898), *A Modern Utopia* (1905), and many other novels. Wells held an optimistic view of the future, with an internationalist perspective, and so his utopias reflected the end of national divisions and the growth of a truly humane civilization, as he saw it. When Huxley read Wells' *Men Like Gods*, he was inspired to make fun of its optimism with his characteristically ironic wit. What began as a parody turned into a novel of its own—*Brave New World*.

The brave new world of Huxley's novel is not a "good place," and so it is not, in the strictest terms, a utopia. Huxley himself called his world a "negative utopia," the opposite of the traditional utopia. Readers have also used the word "dystopia," meaning "bad place," to describe Huxley's fictional world and others like it.

Huxley's dark view of the future opened a new door in fiction and seemed to revive interest in the old traditional utopian form by giving it a modern edge. George Orwell's *Animal Farm* (1946) and *1984* (1949) build on the energy and meaning of their predecessor, *Brave New World*. In *Fahrenheit 451* (1950), science fiction writer Ray Bradbury proposes a future society without history or literature, a dystopia of which Huxley's World Controller Mustapha Mond himself would probably approve.

In the 1960s, Anthony Burgess imagined his own futuristic London in *A Clockwork Orange*, rehearsing the themes of control and the loss of self introduced by Huxley. And Huxley's disturbing views of science and technology have even echoed in Thomas Pynchon's *Gravity's Rainbow* (1973), where the anti-hero, wandering the streets of London during the V-2 raids of World War II, discovers his own dark history of social (and sexual) conditioning.

The Structure of the Novel

As a writer, Huxley refused to be kept to simple, chronological structure in his fiction. He characteristically experiments with structure, surprising his reader by juxtaposing two different conversations or point of view. In *Point Counter Point* (1928), Huxley even attempted to break out of traditional narrative structure altogether—to make fiction imitate the flow of musical counterpoint.

In *Brave New World*, Huxley's plan to create a futuristic world and then to introduce John the Savage as an outsider demanded another kind of unconventional structure. To achieve his effect, Huxley divides the novel roughly into thirds. The first part of the novel establishes the dystopia—the London of the future—with enough detail and background to encourage the reader to accept the world as a given. The second part plunges the reader into a thoroughly different world—the Savage Reservation—to experience the shock of the London characters who are traveling there as tourists. The central part also introduces the real main character, John, in the only world he has known since birth. The third part unfolds the events of John's life in London and his challenge of the dystopia.

Huxley's structuring of *Brave New World* defies the conventions of both mainstream and utopian fiction. In most traditional utopian novels, the utopia itself stands more or less alone as a setting, with no distracting side-trips to other places. The only contrast to the utopia, then, is the reader's own culture and society. But in introducing the Savage Reservation, Huxley introduces another fictional world—a rival and contrast to his dystopia within the novel itself.

According to convention, the inclusion of the Savage Reservation should blur the clarity of the world of London. But Huxley manages to bring his dystopia into even sharper focus with the trip to the Savage Reservation. Both worlds emerge as believable and horrifying, each in its own way.

By holding the introduction of his main character until the middle of the novel, Huxley also flouts narrative convention. In this, Huxley uses the reader's expectations about structure to produce a particular effect. Since convention dictates that the main character appear very early in the novel, readers frequently become convinced that Bernard Marx will be at the center of the plot and theme. Just when Bernard proves himself cowardly and weak, despite his rebelliousness, Huxley offers John, the real main character.

Compared to Bernard, John appears truly heroic, at least initially, and, as a "savage," introduces a new perspective that Huxley uses upon the return to London. In bringing John into a dystopia already familiar to the reader, Huxley can play the reader's knowledge against the character's innocence. And the effect of this irony—Huxley's strong point—intensifies the climax and conclusion of *Brave New World*.

A Brief Synopsis

Brave New World opens in London, nearly six hundred years in the future ("After Ford"). Human life has been almost entirely industrialized—controlled by a few people at the top of a World State.

The first scene, offering a tour of a lab where human beings are created and conditioned according to the society's strict caste system, establishes the antiseptic tone and the theme of dehumanized life. The natural processes of birth, aging, and death represent horrors in this world.

Bernard Marx, an Alpha-Plus (or high-caste) psychologist, emerges as the single discontented person in a world where material comfort and physical pleasure—provided by the drug *soma* and recreational sex—are the only concerns. Scorned by women, Bernard nevertheless manages to engage the attention of Lenina Crowne, a "pneumatic" beauty who agrees to spend a vacation week with him at the remote Savage Reservation in New Mexico, a place far from the controlled, technological world of London.

Before Bernard leaves, his superior, the D.H.C., spontaneously reveals that long ago he, too, visited the Savage Reservation, and he confesses in sorrow that he lost the woman who accompanied him there. Embarrassed by the disclosure of his socially unacceptable emotion, the D.H.C. turns on Bernard, threatening him with banishment for his own social sins—not engaging enthusiastically enough in sex and *soma*.

In the Savage Reservation with Lenina, Bernard meets a woman from London who gave birth to a son about 20 years before. Seeing his opportunity to gain power over the D.H.C.—the father of the child—Bernard brings Linda and John back to London and presents them publicly to the D.H.C., who is about to banish Bernard.

Shocked and humiliated by the proof of his horrifying connection with natural birth, the D.H.C. flees in terror. Once a social outcast, Bernard now enjoys great success, because of his association with the new celebrity—John, called "the Savage."

Reared on the traditional ways of the Reservation and an old volume of the poetry of Shakespeare, John finds London strange, confusing, and finally repellent. His quotation of Miranda's line from *The Tempest*—"O brave new world / That has such people in it"—at first expresses his awe of the "Other Place" his mother told him of as a child. But the quotation becomes ironic as John becomes more and more disgusted by the recreational sex, *soma*, and identical human beings of London.

Lenina's attempted seduction provokes John's anger and violence, and, later, the death of Linda further arouses his fury. At last, John's attempt to keep a crowd of Deltas from their ration of *soma* results in a riot and his arrest, along with Bernard and Helmholtz Watson, an "emotional engineer" who wishes to be a poet.

The three face the judgment of World Controller Mustapha Mond, who acknowledges the flaws of this brave new world, but pronounces the loss of freedom and individuality a small price to pay for stability. Mond banishes Bernard and Helmholtz to the Falkland Islands and rules that John must stay in London.

When his two friends leave for their exile, John determines to make a retreat for himself in a remote, secluded lighthouse outside the city. There he tries to purify himself of civilization with ritual whippings and vomiting.

Drawn by the spectacle of his wild penances, reporters and crowds press in on John, who becomes a public curiosity—a kind of human animal in a zoo. When Lenina appears in the crowd, John furiously attacks her with the whip. John's frenzy inflames the crowd, and, in accordance with their social training, the violence turns into a sexual orgy, with John drawn in more or less unwillingly.

The next day, when John awakes from the effects of the *soma*, he realizes in horror what he has done. The novel closes on an image of John's body, hanging lifeless from a wooden beam in his lighthouse retreat.

List of Characters

Bernard Marx An Alpha-Plus psychologist, rumored to have received alcohol in his blood surrogate, a circumstance that would explain his shortness. Identifying himself as a true individual, Bernard bristles at the social pressures for conformity and longs for the intense, heroic feelings but lacks the ability to be a rebel. He brings John the Savage and Linda back from the Savage Reservation and so makes possible the conflict that informs the last third of the novel.

John the Savage The son born of parents from the brave new world but raised in the Savage Reservation, John represents a challenge to the dystopia. He is the character closest to being the hero of the novel.

Lenina Crowne A technician, attracted by Bernard, in love with John. A conventional young woman who is drawn unconsciously toward danger, she represents ideal beauty for John.

Linda John's mother. An upper-caste Londoner, she commits the ultimate social sin by bearing a child. She is deeply ashamed and longs for escape, finding it in peyote, mescal, sex, and *soma*.

Mustapha Mond The World Controller, intellectually and politically powerful. He offers a historical view of the brave new world at the beginning of the novel and later debates John and Helmholtz on society's values. Mond sentences Bernard and Helmholtz to be banished to the Falkland Islands and determines that John must stay in London.

Helmholtz Watson Bernard's friend, later a friend of John. An Emotional Engineer, he longs to become a poet. He represents a more courageous and intellectual character than Bernard.

The D.H.C. The Director of Hatcheries and Conditioning, called "Tomakin" by Linda. He occupies an important position in the brave new world but loses it when Linda announces that he is the father of their son, John.

Henry Foster An Alpha who is seeing Lenina Crowne. He is a typically conventional Londoner.

Fanny Crowne Lenina's friend. Fanny represents the conventional views of the brave new world. She encourages Lenina to pursue John sexually if he will not take the lead.

Popé Linda's lover in Malpais. Popé's involvement with Linda inspires John's deep revulsion for sex.

Mitsima An old Indian man in Malpais who begins to teach John to mold clay and presides in the marriage ceremony John witnesses. He represents the beginning and end of John's involvement in the traditional life of Malpais.

Character Map

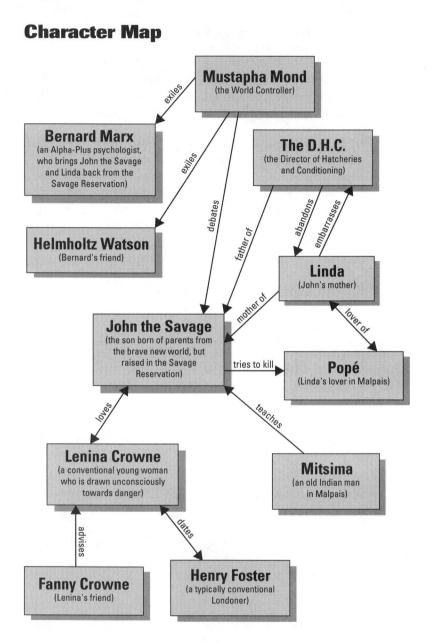

CRITICAL COMMENTARIES

Chapter 1

Summary

The novel opens in the distant future at the Central London Hatchery and Conditioning Centre. This institution plays an essential role in the artificial reproduction and social conditioning of the world's population.

As the chapter begins, the Director of the Centre (the D.H.C.) conducts a group of new students, as well as the reader, on a tour of the facility and its operations—a biological version of the assembly line, with test-tube births as the product. They begin at the Fertilizing Room, move on to the Bottling Room, the Social Predestination Room, and the Decanting Room. Along the way, the D.H.C. explains the basic operation of the plant—Bokanovsky's Process—in which one fertilized egg produces from 8 to 96 "buds" that will grow into identical human beings.

The conditioning that goes along with this process aims to make the people accept and even like their "inescapable social destiny." That destiny occurs within a Caste System (or social hierarchy) ranging from the handsome and intelligent Alpha Pluses down to the working drone Epsilons.

The chapter also introduces two workers at the Centre: Henry Foster, who will figure as a minor character in the story; and "pneumatic" Lenina Crowne, a major character who will affect the destiny of the novel's protagonist.

Commentary

In the reader's first glimpse of the dystopia, Huxley drives home the significance of his futuristic world with the motto "Community. Identity. Stability." All the technology, planning, and conditioning of this World State exist solely to support and maintain these ends.

Theme

The Fordian world does not seem so menacing and sinister as Orwell's *1984*, but the reader can see even in the first chapter that the cheeriness masks a dark reality. Personal identity—perhaps even humanity itself—is strangled by the demands of community and stability.

On the tour, the D.H.C. briskly explains the technology of fertilization—the most intimate human activity—as the carefully calculated, sterile procedure to produce identical people. In a brilliant adaptation of Ford's assembly line, the Central London Hatchery turns out (nearly) interchangeable human beings, who, like the D.H.C. and Henry Foster, can complement one another effortlessly, even to the point of completing each other's sentences.

Theme

Stability requires both the elimination of differences (except with regard to caste) and the end of dissatisfaction. The eugenics lab answers the identity challenge; conditioning manages satisfaction. The D.H.C. announces piously that virtue and goodness spring from the work of the social predestinators, whose job is "making people like their inescapable social destiny." With this statement, Huxley introduces a major theme—the role of choice and even pain in becoming a full human being. The D.H.C.'s dogma will meet a challenge with John, the "uncivilized" character (introduced in Chapter 7).

Style & Language

Huxley employs several narrative techniques to introduce his dystopia in the first chapter. The tour for new students affords a realistic opportunity for Huxley to explain the theories and practices of stability while immersing the reader in the physical world of the dystopia. A brief reference to the Hatchery itself—a "squat" building of "only thirty-four stories"—also gives a sense of the surrounding landscape, a city, by implication, of lofty heights. And, to further orient the reader, Huxley fixes a date—A.F. 632—the number as well as the "A.F." emphasizing the difference between the reader's world and the futuristic world of the novel.

Note especially Huxley's comparison of technology with nature and his point of making technology more alive than nature itself. In the first chapter, Huxley describes the sunlight as cold and dead, except when it hits the tubes of the microscopes, which turn it a buttery, sun-like yellow. In this world, artificiality itself is a kind of power, competing with and augmenting the forces of nature.

Note, too, the inclusion of early twentieth-century prejudices in the dystopia; for example, in the racially charged (and unscientific) comparisons of human ovaries and in the all-male student group. Such details remind the reader that any futuristic fiction reveals as much about a writer's response to the present as hopes or fears for the future.

Glossary

(Here and in the following chapters, difficult words and phrases, as well as allusions and historical references, are explained.)

Alpha, Beta, Gamma, Delta, Epsilon the names of the castes of the dystopia. They are the first five letters of the Greek alphabet, used most commonly in British schools and universities as grades, equivalent to A, B, C, D, and F.

Bokanovsky's Process Huxley's phrase. A method for producing many identical eggs from a single egg. It is the basis for producing identical human beings.

Podsnap's Technique Huxley's phrase. A method for speeding up the ripening of mature eggs. The process makes possible the production of many identical human beings at roughly the same time.

decanting pouring from one container into another. Here, Huxley's term for birth.

freemartin an imperfectly developed female calf, usually sterile. Here, Huxley's term for a sterile woman. Most of the women of the dystopia are freemartins.

surrogate a substitute.

lupus any of various diseases with skin lesions.

demijohn a large bottle of glass or earthenware, with a narrow neck and a wicker casing.

A.F. Huxley's term, following all the dates in the modern era ("After Ford").

Henry Ford (1863–1947) U.S. automobile manufacturer credited with developing interchangeable parts and the assembly-line process. Here, the god-like figure of the dystopia.

lift British word for elevator.

corpus luteum a mass of yellow tissue formed in the ovary by a ruptured graafian follicle that has discharged its ovum; if the ovum is fertilized, this tissue secretes the hormone progesterone, needed to maintain pregnancy.

thyroxin the active hormone of the thyroid gland.

Chapter 2

Summary

The D.H.C. continues his tour of the Centre in the Infant Nursery. Here he lectures the new students on the importance of social conditioning as "*moral* education."

The D.H.C. oversees a demonstration of "Neo-Pavlovian Conditioning." Nurses expose a group of babies to books and flowers and then add a violent explosion, alarm bells, shrieking sirens, and finally an electric shock. This experience, notes the D.H.C., will "unalterably" condition the reflexes of the babies so that they will develop an "instinctive hatred" of books and nature.

According to the D.H.C., such social conditioning ultimately maximizes economic consumption among the population. To illustrate his point, he explains how a dislike of nature can be transformed into a love of country sports—and that involves the consumption of a nearly endless variety of manufactured consumer goods.

The D.H.C. also recounts an anecdote about little Reuben Rabinovitch to discuss "sleep-teaching or hypnopaedia"—the "greatest moralizing and socializing force of all time." By way of an example, the D.H.C. and students look in on a sleep-teaching session on Elementary Class Consciousness.

Commentary

Theme

In this chapter, Huxley continues his presentation of dystopian social stability with a close look at the theory and practice of early conditioning. In the explanation of hypnopaedia and infantile conditioning, Huxley makes clear that the elimination of choice increases economic and social stability but diminishes the potential for human growth.

The price of stability emerges most memorably in the scene in which Delta children—predestined for rote factory work—receive their conditioning to dislike the books and flowers. The image of happy babies crawling toward colorful books and beautiful blooms is filled with conventional sentimentality, but Huxley's reversal with the alarms and electric shock sharpens the reader's response. The reality of the conditioning represents its own legitimate argument against the theory of social, political, and economic stability. Note again Huxley's use of natural imagery as the complement to technology, when the sun beams warmly on the flowers, almost as if offering aid in the conditioning.

Less violent, but nonetheless powerful, hypnopaedia emerges as the source of underlying assumptions and prejudices in the dystopia. The lesson in class consciousness gives each child a social identity but cuts off the possibility of forming friendships outside of caste or even forming opinions of one's own. Throughout the novel, characters spout the sentiments of their hynopaedic training almost unconsciously and behave according to the precepts of the sleep-teaching. Even those—like Bernard Marx—who are conscious of the techniques of hypnopaedia cannot fully escape its power. Again, the dystopian practice supports social stability but destroys personal identity and independence.

The power of words—and responses to particular words—form an important theme in *Brave New World*. Hypnopaedia, Huxley makes clear, uses words at the vulnerable time during sleep to produce unquestioning loyalty or aversion in people. The World State, in effect, whispers into the ear of each of its sleeping young citizens to ensure compliance with the social order. Banned words—especially "mother"—produce a strong response of revulsion and shame, the effect of the carefully taught aversion to human reproduction.

Huxley draws the reader's attention to this fact in a comic turn that forms a memorable part of the students' discussion with the D.H.C. Shocked by the D.H.C.'s frank use of the words "mother" and "father," the students blush and then grin, while Huxley expresses their reactions by substituting the offending words with "crash." As the chapter emphasizes, then, the state's use of language plays an important role in shaping people's consciousness and manipulating their energies toward particular social and economic goals.

Note the change in symbols from the pre-Fordian world. The D.H.C. makes the sign of the T (as opposed to the cross), which the students repeat, in reverence to Henry Ford's Model T automobile, the product of the assembly line. The practiced piety recalls an earlier age, but the meaning of the gesture has changed. The World State has appropriated the Christian symbol and turned it into the Fordian T—significantly by cutting off the top of the cross. Even the symbols of the dystopia make clear the diminishing possibilities for humanity.

Glossary

Neo-Pavlovian Conditioning Huxley's term for the dystopian form of infant training. The term derives from the classical conditioning system named for the Russian physiologist Ivan Petrovich Pavlov (1849–1931).

viscose a substance used in making rayon thread and fabric.

Model T the first car produced on Henry Ford's assembly line.

hypnopaedia sleep-teaching.

asafoetida a bad-smelling gum resin. It was formerly used to treat some illnesses, or, in folk medicine, to repel disease.

viviparous bearing or bringing forth living young, as most mammals and some other animals do.

George Bernard Shaw (1856–1950) British dramatist and critic. Here, one of Huxley's most famous contemporaries, whom he sarcastically singles out for particular mention as an accepted genius of the dystopia.

Chapter 3

Summary

In this chapter, the D.H.C.'s tour moves outside into the garden, where the students watch very young children engaged in sexual games. The D.H.C. tells the students—to their shock—that such erotic play seemed abnormal in the time before Ford.

This chapter also introduces Mustapha Mond—Resident Controller for Western Europe and one of the Ten World Controllers. Mond figures in the novel as a kind of enlightened dictator ("his Fordship"), who understands this brave new world, as well as the old world before Ford.

As the chapter dissolves into a verbal montage, Mond lectures on history—and its suppression—beginning appropriately with Henry Ford's adage: "History is bunk!" Mond recalls a world ravaged by anthrax bombs and poison gases in the Nine Years' War, followed by the great Economic Collapse, and finally the "choice between World Control and destruction." As Mond notes, *soma*, the ubiquitous drug of choice in this brave new world, brought an end to worry, while "stability" proved to be the keystone to social control—the "primal and ultimate need."

The montage becomes more surrealistic as the chapter draws to a close, jumbling mottoes of the World State with snatches of dialogue. For example, it fuses Ford and Freud (in psychological matters), listens in on Lenina chatting with her friend Fanny, and introduces Bernard Marx, who will emerge in subsequent chapters as a major character.

Commentary

In this chapter, Huxley introduces the historical forces that led to the creation of the dystopia. The analysis, delivered by World Controller Mustapha Mond, seems to contradict Ford's own statement, quoted by Mond, "History is bunk." With the appearance of the unconventional, powerful Mond, Huxley offers a deeper, grittier vision of the dystopia than the sanitized explanations of Henry Foster and the D.H.C.

Mond, the only character who knows both the pre-Fordian and Fordian worlds, lectures with passion and detail on the self-destruction of the previous order (the world of the reader) and the building of the World State, the only alternative to chaos. In a series of gory and terrifying images—some, like the booted leg, inspired by the violence of the First World War—Huxley paints the agonized death of the familiar world of democracy and individual freedom. From these ashes, the survivors brought forth what they believed to be the only truly successful framework for living developed in the modern age—Ford's assembly line, with its concept of interchangeable parts, making possible almost limitless production and consumption.

In Fordian times, Mond's lecture makes clear, consumption and the enjoyment of consumption is the primary human activity. The "viviparous" life—the ordinary family—no longer exists, banished by the World State in favor of Conditioning Centres, where decanted children grow up in an environment designed to ensure their loyalty to the social order and (much the same thing) train them to consume appropriately. Here, Mond reminds the students, all their needs are met, all obstacles to happiness removed.

Again, in this chapter, Huxley brings forward the theme of choice and pain as essential parts of human life. If all obstacles are removed, as Mond says, if no one feels passion or pain, what kind of human life is possible? At this point in the novel, Mond presents the life of uninterrupted happiness as the ideal. Later (in Chapters 16–17), Huxley reveals another, more complicated side to the World Controller, when Mond debates on the subject of civilization and its price.

Even now, Huxley dramatizes the emptiness of a life controlled by the consumption of goods and recreational sex. In a surrealistic series of jump-cuts from Mond to the people leaving work, Huxley underlines the purposelessness of the "progress" evident in the dystopia. Violent passion is avoided, but people still need a chemical "Violent Passion Surrogate" once a month. Most women are sterile or practice contraception, yet they must submit to a chemically induced fake pregnancy to maintain their physical and psychological health. Human nature has not changed, obviously; the World State has simply redefined it and compensated for the difference with chemicals.

The most important chemical of all is *soma*, the drug sponsored by the state to reduce or eliminate feelings of unhappiness. Non-toxic, with no after-effects, *soma* is the perfect drug for dulling the senses against any perception of the emptiness of life. *Soma* is, therefore, a powerful, essential tool for social control in the dystopia because it prevents the dissatisfaction and rage that might result in revolution.

Character Insight

Bernard spurns *soma* in disgust, preferring, he explains, to feel his own emotional state, however miserable. In refusing *soma*—the conventional means of remaining perpetually happy—Bernard believes himself to be a rebellious, authentic human being. As the novel progresses, however, Bernard's desire to feel emotion freely will seem less heroic and more adolescent.

Glossary

surreptitious secret, stealthy.

auto-eroticism masturbation.

Our Freud Huxley's phrase. A pious reference to Sigmund Freud (1856–1939), Austrian physician and neurologist: father of psychoanalysis.

flivver a small, cheap automobile, especially an old one. Here, used respectfully to refer to Ford's Model T.

anthrax an infectious disease of wild and domesticated animals, especially cattle and sheep, which is caused by a bacillus and can be transmitted to people.

ectogenesis the growth process of embryonic tissue placed in an artificial environment, as a test tube. Here, the conventional process of birth.

soma an intoxicating plant juice referred to in Indian religious writings. Here, Huxley's term for a powerful calming and hallucinogenic drug without any serious side effects.

boskage a natural growth of trees or shrubs.

pneumatic inflated. Here, Huxley's word describing a woman with a full, shapely figure.

Malthusian drill Huxley's phrase for practicing contraception. From the word "Malthusian," referring to the theory developed by English economist Thomas Malthus (1766–1834), that the world population tends to increase faster than the food supply with inevitable disastrous results unless natural restrictions, such as war, famine, and disease, reduce the population or the increase is checked by moral restraint.

Chapter 4

Summary

This chapter opens on an elevator where Lenina sees Bernard. She wants to talk with him about their planned trip to New Mexico, but he seems hesitant. In fact, Bernard wants to express his feelings to her, but when he tries, Lenina fails to notice. She's late for a date with Henry Foster.

As Lenina and Henry take off in their helicopter for the date, their trip offers a panoramic view of London and its suburbs. It unfolds as a miniature version of this futuristic world—from Charing-T Tower to Hounslow Feely Studios to the Obstacle Golf Course.

The second half of the chapter returns to Bernard, who feels inadequate. Although an Alpha Plus, Bernard worries over his short stature (due, apparently, to a mistake during his decanting as a test-tube embryo). Because of this, he feels like a social "outsider": "I am I, and wish I wasn't."

Bernard flies to Propaganda House to meet his friend, Helmholtz Watson, who writes state propaganda as an Emotional Engineer. Despite his overpowering stature and success with women, Watson, too, feels "all alone," because he has "too much ability." As a result, he senses a kinship with Bernard—the knowledge they share that they are "individuals."

Commentary

Here Huxley offers a contrast of two important and very different characters: Bernard, the Alpha-Plus psychologist; and Lenina, the Gamma technician.

Character Insight

As an Alpha Plus, at the top of society's strict caste system, Bernard should be enjoying every benefit of his society especially reserved for the elite—including relative freedom. The other Alphas—the D.H.C. and Henry Foster, for example—move through the futuristic world with confidence and gusto. Even the unconventional Mustapha Mond seems happy, in his own way. Bernard, however, lives in a state of misery, anxious and angry; short for his caste, he faces ridicule from women, insubordination from inferiors, and exclusion from the cheery intimacy of social life among his equals.

Bernard at once longs for and scorns the joys of his world. Infatuated with Lenina, he dreams of a vacation alone with her but flinches when she mentions it in public. Sexually obsessed, Bernard lingers over Lenina's beauty but is repulsed by the conventional (for this world) attitude she exhibits.

Bernard may be a misfit, but he shows little of the true rebel's conviction and seriousness of purpose. When Bernard seeks the company of Helmholtz Watson, another Alpha who is dissatisfied with life, Huxley offers a new view on his character by contrast. Although popular and socially successful in the ways Bernard is not, Helmholtz nevertheless longs for some meaning in his life and work. Helmholtz's discontent, Huxley stresses, is on a higher plane than Bernard's. In contrast to Helmholtz, Bernard seems merely childish and whiny. In later chapters, Huxley sharpens this distinction between these two unhappy Alphas and constructs a common resolution for them both.

Lenina, on the other hand, appears comfortable in the dystopia. Despite her daring experiment with her long-standing relationship with Henry Foster, she is conventional by the standards of her world—cheery, unthinking, and infantile. In her talk with Bernard, she displays all the unembarrassed enthusiasm for sex that hypnopaedia and social life have taught her since childhood. Still, her choice of Bernard seems somehow rebellious, revealing an underlying, yet not fully recognized, dissatisfaction.

One brief, but significant scene occurs on the roof with the Epsilon elevator operator. In earlier chapters, the Alphas who control the predestination of fetuses and the conditioning of infants maintain that the members of every caste are happy, in their own ways. The sudden yearning expressed by the lowly Epsilon in his longing cry—"Roof! . . . Oh, roof!"— reveals for an instant that conditioning cannot completely remove the human need for air, space, and beauty. There is a similar scene in Fritz Lang's futuristic film *Metropolis* (1927), in which a woman and children from the underground world suddenly glimpse the richness and beauty of the upper world through opened elevator doors. In both works, the scenes dramatize the unspoken injustice of the social hierarchy by bringing the lowest and the highest face to face, creating the conflict that convention seeks to avoid.

Glossary

parathyroid any of usually four small, oval glands on or near the thyroid gland; they secret a hormone important in the control of the calcium-phosphorus balance of the body.

Charing-T Tower Huxley's re-creation of a London train station, Charing Cross Station.

simian of or like an ape or monkey. Here, used to describe the Epsilon elevator operator.

Chapter 5

Summary

This chapter opens with Lenina and Henry taking off in their helicopter when the Obstacle Golf Course closes. They pass over Burnham Beeches—a satirical allusion to Shakespeare—and then the Slough Crematorium. As they discuss death and "phosphorus recovery"—"we can go on being socially useful even after we're dead"—Lenina reveals her class prejudices, especially against Epsilons.

They fly to Westminster Abbey Cabaret, where they dance the evening away to the Malthusian Blues. Despite the *soma* they consume, Lenina remembers her contraception in preparation for a night of pneumatic sex.

The second half of the chapter follows Bernard as he flies past the chiming Big Henry—the Fordian version of Big Ben—to the Fordson Community Singery. There he participates—without really believing—in a kind of religious service that includes such rituals as the sign of the T, blessed *soma*, and solidarity hymns. Under the influence of the sacramental *soma*, the ceremony dissolves into an "orgy-porgy" of sex.

But while the others find the "calm ecstasy of achieved consummation," Bernard feels only more isolated in his "separateness"—"much more alone, indeed, more hopelessly himself than he had ever been in his life before."

Commentary

In this chapter, Huxley introduces the dystopian combination of religion and sex, featuring a date in a cathedral/cabaret juxtaposed with a spiritual ritual that ends in an orgy.

Henry and Lenina's dinner and dancing evening emphasizes the artificiality of their world. The night is clear and starry, but they are unaware of the stars at all because of the overpowering electric sky-signs that light up London. In this point, Huxley's response to his own era—artificial light already dominating the city night—strongly influences his ideas about the futuristic world.

Inside Westminster Abbey Cabaret—the new use for the historical, venerable site where English kings and queens were once crowned— the domed ceiling offers another sky altogether: a tropical sunset. Perception is also modified by the *soma* served at dinner so that everyone and everything seems delightful. Even the music is synthetic—a proudly advertised feature of the cabaret. Emotions, music, scenery—all the elements of romance come already engineered by the state.

The evening ends, as conventionally it should, with recreational, non-productive sex. Huxley closes the chapter before describing Henry and Lenina's love-making, but leaves the reader to infer that it will be just as artificial and manipulated as the rest of the evening.

Bernard's "orgy-porgy" Solidarity Service—the biweekly pseudo-religious meeting—parallels in many ways Lenina's date with Henry. Music and *soma* play important parts in the evening, enhancing mood and eliminating any inhibitions. On their date, Lenina and Henry's *soma* serves as a kind of after-dinner brandy, while it becomes, in the Solidarity Service, a surrogate for the bread and wine of the Christian Eucharist. In the service, *soma* and sex represent union with a Greater Being and with each other.

Note especially the cries of the participants when they hear the "feet of the Greater Being" as he approaches. Huxley draws on the tradition of the revival meeting here, and he also underscores the similarity between religious ecstasy and sexual excitement—a point completed when the service turns to orgy.

"Orgy-porgy"—the conventional close of the Solidarity Service— uses group sex as a method of breaking down the perceived differences between people and so increasing social stability. What might once have been the spontaneous expression of sexual feeling—even an act of rebellion—becomes here merely another mandatory state activity.

Just as in Westminster Abbey Cabaret, the music at the Solidarity Service sets the pace, initiates feeling, and manipulates actions. Again, Huxley lets the artificial atmosphere descend to control the characters in the rituals of the dystopia.

Note, too, Lenina and Henry's lip service to the worth of every individual. The belief (hypnopaedia at work) allows upper-caste members of the society to disregard the truth about the deliberately arrested development of the Gammas, Deltas, and Epsilons that serve them. Epsilons do not mind being Epsilons, Henry and Lenina tell each other, because they know nothing else. Huxley has already offered a brief view of the longing in lower-caste people, with the Epsilon elevator operator in Chapter 4.

Glossary

Westminster Abbey Gothic church (originally a Benedictine abbey) where English monarchs are crowned; it is also a burial place for English monarchs, famous statesmen and writers, etc. Here, the site of the Westminster Abbey cabaret, or nightclub.

orgy-porgy Huxley's term for a ritual sexual orgy, from the children's nursery rhyme, "Georgy-Porgy."

detumescence a decrease in swelling.

diminuendo a decrease in volume.

plagently loudly and with resonance.

Chapter 6

Summary

As this chapter opens, Lenina worries about Bernard's eccentric desire for privacy and his tendency to question basic social assumptions. She thinks him "odd."

In a flashback to their first date, Lenina and Bernard quarrel when he hovers their helicopter over the English Channel so that they can observe the power of Nature. Bernard wants an adult—and emotional—relationship with Lenina, not just the mindless sex that consummates their first date.

In the middle section of the chapter, Bernard submits his travel to the D.H.C., who remembers his own holiday many years earlier to the Savage Reservation. The D.H.C. tells Bernard about the young woman he took on his trip and how she disappeared mysteriously during their stay on the Reservation.

Embarrassed by his emotional reverie, the D.H.C. shifts attention by expressing his disappointment in Bernard's odd behavior outside work and threatens to exile him to Iceland. But this threat has a tonic effect on Bernard, who later boasts about it to his friend Helmholtz, who likes Bernard but hates his boasting and self-pity.

In the third section, Bernard and Lenina fly to Sante Fe, where they meet with the Warden of the Reservation. As the Warden leers at Lenina and describes the Reservation—there's no escape, and human birth remains a reality—Bernard suddenly remembers that he left the eau de cologne tap running at home.

When Bernard calls Helmholtz about the tap, Watson gives him some bad news: the D.H.C. intends to exile Bernard to Iceland. Appalled by the news, Bernard's "theoretical courage" evaporates, and Lenina persuades him to take *soma* to calm himself before they fly off to the Savage Reservation.

Commentary

In Chapter 6, Huxley reveals Bernard's pained recognition of the consequences of his anti-social feelings and actions. The chapter further clarifies Bernard's very shallow attempts to be an individual and makes clear that he lacks the moral courage to suffer for freedom.

Up to now, Bernard has expressed his longing to feel something—anything—strongly. Since passion is dangerous to social stability, the very thought of feeling intensely constitutes blasphemy, as the shocked Lenina points out. All the conventions of this society—*soma* consumption, regular recreational sex—are designed to prevent strong feelings like rage and prolonged sexual desire from building up in emotional power. So far, Bernard has experimented with passion by avoiding *soma* and nursing his anger, but in this chapter, he learns about actual, unavoidable strong feelings—first at a distance, then very personally.

The D.H.C.'s shared memories of losing the young woman he was traveling with in the New Mexico reservation represent a dangerous disclosure. In spontaneously confessing his anxiety and remorse over the woman's disappearance, the D.H.C. comes perilously close to admitting that he loved her—a shocking social sin. The D.H.C.'s memory, still powerful enough to give him dreams, is Bernard's first close contact with an authentic emotional experience. But Bernard responds with a characteristically adolescent reaction; instead of responding sympathetically, he cringes and leers, at once fascinated and repulsed by the possibility of a superior's vulnerability.

Character Insight

The chapter also features Bernard's first personal experience of intense feelings, following his discovery that the D.H.C. intends to transfer him to a remote sub-station in Iceland for his lack of conventional "infantile decorum." Suddenly thrown into a genuine crisis, the kind of trial he has been longing for in preference to the soothing *soma*-induced tranquility of everyday life, Bernard panics, his courage gone without a trace. Like any other citizen of the dystopia, he swallows *soma* against the harsh realities facing him and, in that gesture, proves his supposed rebellion to be a shallow, cowardly farce.

Literary Device

Note that in introducing the Savage Reservation, Huxley employs the Warden as a kind of guide, like Henry Foster and the D.H.C. in the first two chapters. Like Bernard and Lenina, the reader becomes a tourist, about to enter yet another part of Huxley's fictional world.

Glossary

brachycephalic having a relatively short or broad head.

Chapter 7

Summary

With their Indian guide, Bernard and Lenina enter the Savage Reservation. Lenina finds everything here "queer."

Lenina soon discovers that she has forgotten her *soma*, so she must experience the Indian village of Malpais as an unmedicated reality. In quick succession, she and Bernard witness old age in the figure of an ancient Indian, Indian mothers nursing their babies, and a hedonistic ritual dance that fuses Christian and Indian religion. This wild dance ends with a coyote-masked shaman whipping a young man until he collapses—a blood sacrifice to bring the rain and make the corn grow.

After this bloody spectacle, Bernard and Lenina meet a straw-haired, blue-eyed young man dressed—incongruously, it seems—as an Indian. Strangely, too, the young man speaks like a character from Shakespeare and tells them that his mother—Linda—comes from the "Other Place." When he also mentions that his father was named "Tomakin," Bernard connects this young man with the D.H.C.'s visit to the Reservation.

The young savage introduces them to Linda—a "very stout blonde squaw," who tells Lenina and Bernard her strange story of being abducted by the Indians. She has spent much of her life on the Reservation, she explains, where she gave birth to her son, John, the young savage.

Commentary

In this chapter, Huxley opens another part of his dystopian world—the Savage Reservation—contrasting it implicitly and explicitly with the world of London, where the rest of the novel is set.

In one sense, Malpais represents the opposite of the rest of the dystopia, an "uncivilized" place against which the reader—as well as tourists Bernard and Lenina—can gauge the imagined progress of the "civilized" world. Here, on the Savage Reservation, age changes people unchecked by chemicals and hormones; women give birth and breast-feed their babies; and the natural process of decay produces sights and smells that appall the sensitive Lenina. In fact, "Civilization is Sterilization" underscores most of Lenina's experience in the Reservation. Fordian London is so clean that birth and old age have been swept away entirely, like germ-producing bacteria. But in Malpais, the pains of birth and death exist and endure unconquered—still the essential facts of human life.

Lenina faces these facts most dramatically in her meeting with Linda, who seems her mirror-double, the woman she might have been under different circumstances. (Note, for example, the similarity between the names "Lenina" and "Linda.") Linda's unspeakable fate—to become a mother and to grow old—is nothing less than a horror, an obscenity, really, to a Fordian mind. As an object of blasphemy and revulsion, Linda represents enormous power, one that Bernard will use in a later chapter to regain his position, just as he will use Linda's son, John, to improve his social standing.

The reader should note Huxley's careful description of the flagellation ritual, a religious ceremony to ensure a good food crop. Lenina finds the incessant drumming very familiar—just like a lower-caste community sing—and her recognition draws attention to the underlying similarities between civilized and uncivilized worlds. In both worlds, music can suspend inhibition and drive people to unity and to action (recall, for example, Bernard's Solidarity Service). Whether dressed in rough wool or shiny viscose, Huxley reveals, people are still people, open and vulnerable to powerful suggestion. Communities of all sorts—whether in Malpais or in London—use similar methods to enforce conformity and so promote social stability.

Note especially the introduction of John, the outsider born on the reservation who emerges as a contrast to Bernard in rebellious thought. Huxley dramatizes the conflict that will develop between John and the expectations of the "Other Place" in his first exchange with Lenina, a bizarre trading of Shakespearean verse and hypnopaedic suggestion. From this chapter onward, John and his struggle become the focus of the novel.

Glossary

treble high-pitched or shrill.

Octoroon a person who has one black great-grandparent.

Good-morrow old-fashioned greeting, used in Shakespeare's time, to mean "good day."

mescal a colorless alcoholic liquor of Mexico made from pulque or other fermented agave juice.

peyote a small, spineless cactus of northern Mexico and the southwestern United States, with rounded stems whose buttonlike tops are chewed, specifically in religious ceremonies by Mexican Indians, for their hallucinogenic effects.

Chapter 8

Summary

In this chapter, John recounts his life on the Reservation to Bernard. Bernard senses how strange and exotic such a life is, as compared to his own experiences. Indeed, he feels as if he and John "were living on different planets, in different centuries."

John's earliest memories involve his mother's relationships with Indian men—especially Popé, who also introduces Linda to the powerful hallucinogenic drug mescal (which she finds similar to soma). John also remembers how the Indian women beat Linda, because she felt no sexual restraints with their men.

As John grows, Linda teaches him to read. Popé finds an old volume of Shakespeare, and the young boy studies it. In fact, John's reading in Shakespeare inspires him to try to kill Popé, who is in bed with Linda. As an adolescent, John is not allowed to undergo the initiation ritual into adult Indian society like the other boys. Instead, John goes out alone into the wilderness where he contrives his own physical trials to enter adulthood. His self-torture gives him a vision of "Time and Death and God."

As John finishes his story, he and Bernard realize that they share the same feelings of being "terribly alone." Suddenly inspired, Bernard invites John—and Linda, too—to return with him to London. In response, John quotes Shakespeare: "O brave new world . . ."

Commentary

Character Insight

In this chapter, Huxley explores the character of John, the child born unexpectedly in the Savage Reservation. A genetic Fordian raised in Malpais, John represents the potential combination of civilization and tradition, but his life has been lonely and heartbreaking. John is the true individual Bernard sometimes longs to be, and, as Huxley makes clear here, being truly individual means living in pain. Because of his European appearance and his mother's sexual activity, John suffers rejection and humiliation at the hands of the elders of Malpais as well as his peers. Banned from initiation into manhood, John has nowhere to turn for help in his growth. An old volume of Shakespeare's plays becomes his guide to life. In the world of poetry and imagination, John's spirit expands, gaining a unique although eccentric strength and vitality.

Implicitly, Huxley compares the memorable, poetic phrases of Shakespeare's poetry with hypnopaedia's catchy lines. John absorbs Shakespeare's poetry in a dream-like state, not entirely understanding the words but receiving the message through repetition, just as the young sleepers of the dystopia accept hypnopaedic wisdom. In both cases, the words form perception, shape behavior, and even inspire direct action. Reading and meditating on Hamlet's rage at his mother's sexual relations, for example, impels John to express his passion in a violent attack on Popé—a failed attempt that nonetheless marks the beginning of John's independent, adult life.

The chapter includes the first appearance of the quotation from *The Tempest* that gives Huxley's novel its title: "O brave new world / That has such people in it." The difference between John's awe of the wonderful "Other Place" and the reader's own knowledge of the dystopia produces powerful dramatic irony at a crucial point. The irony of the phrase not only hints at the disappointment that awaits John but draws the novel together for the reader as well, giving a coherent focus to Huxley's satire. In later chapters, John himself will repeat this phrase, as a means of expressing his changing reactions to the world of London—the reality behind the fairy-tale "Other Place" his mother once described to him.

Note especially in this chapter John's own experience of conditioning, different in kind but not in essence from the conditioning of infants and children in London. John associates the reality of sex, for instance, with the absence of his mother, fear, humiliation, and intense physical pain. This conditioning (accidental, but powerful) occurs early in his life, first when Popé pushes him out of the bedroom, then when the women violently whip Linda and him, and finally when the boys mock him for his mother's sexual freedom. As a result, John displays a strong, persistent aversion to sex, despite his longing for Lenina. Again, Huxley makes the point that all people—civilized or uncivilized—are vulnerable to powerful suggestion.

Chapter 9

Summary

While Lenina takes a *soma*-holiday, Bernard makes the necessary arrangements to bring John and Linda back to London. He flies to Sante Fe where he telephones Mustapha Mond for permission and then meets with the Warden.

During Bernard's trip, John breaks into the Rest House, thinking that Bernard and Lenina have left for London without him. Inside, John discovers Lenina's suitcase and looks through her clothes—including her zippicamiknicks.

When John finds Lenina fast asleep, he thinks of Shakespeare's Juliet. He reaches out to touch her—perhaps even to unzip her zippypajamas with a single pull—but stops himself, thinking: "Detestable thought!"

John retreats when he hears the humming of Bernard's returning helicopter.

Commentary

In this very short chapter, Huxley presents two of his principal characters—Bernard and John—in unexpected, exciting situations of power. The quick view of each character affords the reader an opportunity to compare the men in similar circumstances. Predictably, Bernard proves himself to be a shameless opportunist, while John reveals the complex, mixed feelings of his idealism.

Character Insight

Looking forward to revenging himself on the D.H.C. by bringing Linda and their son back to London, Bernard positively beams with triumph, making his arrangements with masterly briskness and efficiency. His patronizing tone and his expectations of deference contrast sharply with his usual hesitancy. Here Huxley hints that Bernard—with power already gone to his head—will become an unbearable phony, destined ultimately for a great fall.

John's visit to the sleeping, *soma*-tized Lenina contrasts with Bernard's scene in tone. The mood here is a child-like wonder as John explores Lenina's clothes and cosmetics and is ecstatically bathed in her scent. John's approach to the bed where Lenina lies continues the mood of wonder and enchantment. Speaking in Shakespeare's poetry, looking upon her with awe and longing, John seems a character in a fairy tale—a figure in an ideal landscape.

Character Insight

John's hesitancy to pull at Lenina's zipper seems chivalrous in this context, an expression of respect and poetic delicacy. Still, the scene recalls John's early conditioning against sex and the possibility that John is not merely restrained but repressed in sexual matters. With John's sudden suppression of sexual curiosity, Huxley deliberately breaks the romantic mood, introducing the jarring, comic image of his character shaking his head "with the gesture of a dog shaking its ears as it emerges from the water." John is not an ideal knight, Huxley points out, but a young man raised as an outsider in the harsh conditions of Malpais and haphazardly educated by the example of his displaced mother, the legends of the elders, and the poetry of Shakespeare. Nothing in Malpais or London will ever be simple to such a complex, conflicted character.

Glossary

agaves plants of the agave family, such as the century plant.

zippicamiknicks Huxley's word for one-piece underwear for women.

Chapter 10

Summary

Back at the Bloomsbury Centre, the D.H.C. waits with Henry Foster to humiliate Bernard. He plans to publicly confront Bernard in the Fertilizing Room, with its many high-caste workers.

When Bernard arrives, the D.H.C. announces in front of everyone his intention to transfer Bernard to a "Sub-Centre of the lowest order." The D.H.C. explains that Bernard has "grossly betrayed the trust imposed in him"—and that his unorthodox attitudes and behavior threaten Society.

Bernard responds by bringing in Linda, whose appearance—sagging and discolored with age—horrifies and astonishes the crowd. She immediately recognizes the D.H.C. as her "Tomikin" and tells him that he caused her to have a baby—to be a mother. An "appalling hush" fills the room at the mere mention of this "smutty" word.

When John enters and calls the D.H.C. "my father," laughter breaks out among the crowd. Completely humiliated, the D.H.C. rushes from the room.

Commentary

This short chapter features the reversal of fortune that sets into motion the events that dominate the rest of the novel.

The D.H.C.'s plan to chastise Bernard publicly before banishing him for his unorthodox behavior is, the Director maintains, a necessity for social stability, but the D.H.C.'s pious protectiveness of the social order masks his real reason for punishing Bernard—concern about Bernard's revealing his unconventional feelings for Linda. In making an example of Bernard for his behavior, then, the D.H.C. is being hypocritical.

Bernard's dramatic introduction of the middle-aged Linda and her son—the horrifying proof of the D.H.C.'s social sins—represents a brilliant counter-attack, a public humiliation that undercuts the D.H.C.'s moral authority to punish Bernard. The vision of the pompous and hypocritical D.H.C. suddenly shocked into silent terror and revulsion makes the victory a satisfying one for the reader, despite Bernard's characteristic falseness and vindictiveness. In later chapters, Bernard will reap the reward of this masterful surprise, not only avoiding punishment but improving his social status.

The return home does not come up to either Linda's or John's high expectations, however. Linda's appearance—aging, bloated, coarse from hard living without chemical enhancement—seems to be the ultimate punishment for becoming a mother, and the assembled workers shrink from her in horror. John's heartfelt declaration, on his knees before the D.H.C.—"My father!"—incites only uncontrollable laughter among the workers. The scene makes clear that Linda will never be accepted back into the society of Fordian London, but that John may be welcomed as an exotic curiosity. Young and handsome, he conforms to Fordian expectations, while offering the possibility of surprise and sexual interest as well.

Note how Huxley returns the action to London with a few descriptive references to familiar surroundings—the Social Predestination Room, the Nurseries, and at last the Fertilizing Room, where the scene takes place. The descriptions remind the reader of the essential difference between Malpais and London—natural birth versus the bottling and decanting of fetuses—and prepares for the revelation of Linda and her son, the actual, physical reality that the Fertilizing Room is designed to replace.

Glossary

voluptuous sexually attractive because of a full, shapely figure.

undulation a swaying motion. Here, describing Linda's sexually provocative entrance into the Fertilizing Room.

scatological having to do with excrement or excretion.

obliquity a turning aside from moral conduct or sound thinking.

Chapter 11

Summary

As the chapter opens, the D.H.C. has resigned because of the scandal, and Linda has slipped into a permanent *soma*-holiday. She is taking ever higher dosages that will eventually lead to her death.

Bernard suddenly finds himself popular because all upper-caste London wants to see John the Savage. Bernard boasts to Helmholtz about his sexual conquests and lectures Mustapha Mond in a report—offending both of them.

John, meanwhile, experiences a growing disillusionment with this "Brave New World" (as he quotes Shakespeare). He vomits during a tour of a Fordian factory and discovers on his visit to Eton that the library there contains no Shakespeare. He also goes on a date with Lenina to a feely—which he compares unfavorably to *Othello*.

At the end of the date, John disappoints Lenina, dropping her off at her apartment without staying for sex. He feels unworthy of her, while she is confused and frustrated.

Commentary

In this chapter, Huxley features John's discovery of the activities that come closest to imagination and poetry in the world of Fordian London—taking *soma* and going to the feelies.

Huxley has introduced the effects of *soma* very early in the novel, and so the reader is not surprised to find Linda on a more or less perpetual *soma* holiday now that the drug is available to her once more. *Soma*, however, is new to John, and his worry about the drug shortening his mother's life gives Huxley the opportunity to expand on *soma* once again. In explaining what he regards as *soma*'s benefits, Dr. Shaw uses the word "eternity"—a concept John recognizes from Shakespeare's poetry. The moment represents a rare connection for the displaced character.

The chapter also offers a detailed description of the feelies, the popular entertainment that combines the senses of smell and touch in a movie format. Bernard, the reader recalls, disdained the feelies as beneath his intellectual dignity. Huxley's presentation of John's experience, however, makes clear the strengths and weaknesses of the form, which Mustapha Mond describes in Chapter 16 as "practically nothing but pure sensation."

As the chapter reveals, the feelies exist simply to soothe and titillate the senses, while leaving the mind (or, rather, one's conditioning) untouched. The story is pornographic, but conservative, containing nothing at all to introduce doubts into a viewer's sense of social order.

The reader should note the racially charged assumptions underlying Huxley's satire of the feelies, the plot revolving around a black man's abduction and rape of a white woman. Again, the satire tells the reader as much about Huxley's present world as it does the futuristic, fictional world. The technology is different, but the prejudice remains. Note also John's later comparison of the feely he sees with *Othello*, whose tragic hero, John recalls, is also a black man.

The erotic power of the feelies shocks John deeply, because his own unintentional conditioning and poetic education mark off sex as a dangerous, filthy territory. In contrast, Lenina responds enthusiastically to the stimulation and is hurt and confused by John's refusal to end their evening together with sex. The experience drives John back to Shakespeare—the world he understands—and further isolates him from the civilized people of London.

Character Insight

Compared with John—now called "the Savage"—Bernard appears shallow in his supposed individuality and his protests. Reaping the social rewards of his association with a celebrity, Bernard pushes for power and attention. At last popular with women because of his connection to John, Bernard forgets his earlier objections to recreational sex and throws himself into promiscuity with real enthusiasm. He flaunts his unconventional views in public for the mere sensation of risk-taking and even dares to lecture Mustapha Mond in his reports on John. The disapproving comments of his superiors forewarn of Bernard's ultimate fall from social grace.

Bernard's heady experience of power and popularity contrasts sharply with John's growing disillusionment. Note especially John's repetition of the "brave new world" quotation, now deeply ironic, as he views a factory filled with Bokanovsky groups and vomits in disgust.

Glossary

Ariel a character from Shakespeare's *The Tempest*. Shakespeare describes him as a "airy spirit," with magical powers.

prognathous having jaws that project beyond the upper face.

Penitentes members of a penitential religious sect who whip themselves to express remorse for sin and in hope of forgiveness. Here, the spiritual men of John's Malpais home.

Etonians students of Eton College, the most prestigious of British preparatory schools.

vitrified changed into glass by heat.

Arch-Community-Songster of Canterbury Huxley's term describing the dystopia's equivalent for the Archbishop of Canterbury, primate of the Church of England.

Capriccio a musical composition in various forms, usually lively and whimsical in spirit. Here, the term is used in describing the scent organ.

arpeggios the playing of notes of a chord in quick succession instead of simultaneously. Here, again, the musical term is used to describe the scent organ.

Chapter 12

Summary

Disgusted with the brave new world, John refuses to attend a party for the Arch Community Singster of Canterbury. This embarrasses Bernard and destroys his newly won popularity.

Meeting with John and Bernard, Helmholtz reads an anti-social poem he has composed. This reading inspires John to read Shakespeare aloud. Helmholtz's initial delight at the poetic language turns to laughter and ridicule when Shakespeare's ideas about love and sex clash with Helmholtz's own social conditioning.

Commentary

Theme

John's preference for Shakespeare over the feelies leads to an explicit discussion of the power of words to create and express emotion—and to upset the social equilibrium. The chapter also dramatizes John's rejection of Bernard for the more philosophical Helmholtz.

Character Insight

In defying Bernard's demands for him to appear at a very important social gathering, John uses two techniques of resistance—retreat and the Zuni language—both expressing his indifference to and independence from the powerful people of the London world. Faced with demand to behave as a conventional celebrity to ensure Bernard's continued social success, John returns to his Malpais identity, speaking Zuni and seeking comfort in the poetry of Shakespeare. Bernard's helplessness and John's angry disillusion will grow in the coming chapters—creating the climax and bringing about the events of the conclusion.

The main idea of the chapter comes into focus, however, with Helmholtz's surprising composition of a real poem, as opposed to the slogans and catchy phrases he usually creates as a writer of hypnopaedia and feely scenarios. The theme of the poem—solitude—reveals dangerous anti-social leanings (promptly reported to the authorities) and opens the possibility of a poetic response from John—a reading from Shakespeare.

Helmholtz's delight and fascination hint that the "emotional engineer" may be able to respond to and even compose the real poetry he feels compelled to try. Huxley holds the exciting possibility before the reader—then suddenly whisks it away with Helmholtz's loud guffaw at the verses from *Romeo and Juliet*.

Helmholtz's ability to enjoy Shakespeare goes only so far. After that point, Helmholtz's conditioning takes over, preventing him from sharing the imaginative vision offered by the poetry. The failure to connect with real poetry—and with John—brings the chapter to a sad conclusion: the image of a potentially free, potentially poetic individual suddenly reined in by the conditioned narrowness of mind and heart.

Note here Mustapha Mond's regretful censorship of a work he finds interesting, but socially dangerous. Mond's mixed feelings about the responsibility of his authority are revealed further in Chapters 16 and 17.

Note, too, Lenina's growing melancholy as John continues to avoid her. Unfamiliar with real emotion, Lenina can only compare her authentic unhappiness with the chemically induced feelings of a Violent Passion Surrogate. Unconsciously, Lenina's natural emotions lead her into the behavior associated with romantic love in the present world, as when she gazes at the moon.

Huxley also draws a dramatic contrast between John's restraint and the Arch-Community Songster's guiltless enthusiasm for sex with Lenina. Unlike John, the Arch-Community Songster pulls vigorously at Lenina's zipper, ironically topped with the Fordian T, symbol of all that is holy and conventional in the dystopia.

Glossary

Lambeth Palace the official residence in London of the Archbishop of Canterbury since 1197. Here, the home of the Arch-Community-Songster of Canterbury.

St. Helena a small island in the South Atlantic Ocean, off the coast of Africa. It was Napoleon's prison after his defeat by the British. Here, one of the many islands where Mustapha Mond sends people who challenge the World State.

Chapter 13

Summary

Frustrated by John's shyness, Lenina determines to take the sexual lead with "the Savage." When John addresses her with the formality of Malpais tradition and Shakespearean poetry, the confused Lenina simply undresses and approaches him directly. Horrified by Lenina's sexual freedom, John pushes her away, threatening to kill the "impudent strumpet." Lenina retreats in fear.

The chapter ends with a phone call for John with the news that his mother is dying.

Commentary

In this chapter, Lenina determines to approach John for sex directly, rather than continuing to wait for him to take her. In her attempted seduction, Lenina uncovers a disturbingly violent side to John.

So far in London, John has appeared quaint, innocent, and—with the exception of his refusal to join Bernard's party—agreeable. Lenina, who is eager for sex with "the Savage" experiences frustration but interprets John's indifference as simple shyness, which she can overcome by taking a firm hand with him. The possibility that John's sexual restraint is the expression of his own deeply held values and beliefs never occurs to her.

Character Insight

Lenina's frustration recalls the incident in Chapter 3 when a student remembers having to wait a month before a young woman would have sex with him. The emotional intensity was "horrible," just like Lenina's longing, but the passion ended with sexual relief. In taking the sensible Fanny's advice to force the issue with John—and thus get her anti-social feelings over with—Lenina expects the same relief. Conditioned to think of sex as recreational and relationships as fluid and changing, Lenina does not recognize that her curiosity, attraction, and regard for John is, in fact, a serious infatuation that may become love.

The resulting seduction scene is a farce, with neither Lenina nor John knowing what the other is really thinking or feeling. Lenina's plan is straightforward—a direct invitation, undressing, a few lines of a love song, and sex will most certainly follow. But John's view of romance takes a more complex form. Both the traditions of Malpais and the poetry of Shakespeare demand a period of trials, an enforced labor, that will earn the lover the right to marry his beloved.

But trials, labor, and marriage have no meaning in the dystopia. In continuing her sexual approach, Lenina unknowingly steps outside the boundaries that John's education have set down for a worthy women. In John's eyes, if Lenina is not a prize to be won through suffering, then she must be a whore—a "strumpet" to be scorned.

John's early experience has taught him to associate sex with violence, and his conditioning suddenly takes over as his romantic vision of Lenina disappears. As he shakes her violently, slaps and threatens to kill her, he mutters Shakespeare's most passionate verses about unfaithful women, the "drums and music" of the fierce poetry goading him on in his fury. Again, Huxley underlines the relationship of music with the disappearance of inhibition and the expression of strong emotion. John's outburst here looks forward to his later violent passions after leaving London—especially the "atonement" that ends in his death.

Glossary

strumpet prostitute.

fitchew a polecat or weasel. John's quotation of Shakespeare refers to the popular tradition of the fitchew's enthusiasm for mating.

civet a yellowish, fatty substance with a musklike scent, secreted by a gland near the genitals of the civet cat and used in making some perfumes. Here, John quotes Shakespeare's sarcastic use of the term to mean a sweet scent. Pure civet is foul-smelling.

usurp to take or assume by force or without right.

Chapter 14

Summary

In this chapter, John goes to the Park Lane Hospital for the Dying to be with Linda at her death. Music, scents, telescreens, and an unending supply of *soma* fill the ward, while Delta children romp among the beds, learning to view death as pleasant and useful rather than something to be feared.

The children annoy John, making it impossible for him to speak with his dying mother. When Linda wakes from a soma dream and mistakes her son for Popé, John's misery turns to fury. At the moment of death, Linda's terrified eyes seem a reproach to her son. John leaves the hospital angry and distraught.

Commentary

The chapter offers a detailed description of the conventional manner of dying in the dystopia, while dramatizing John's very different expectations at the deathbed of his mother, Linda.

In the early chapters, Henry Foster, the D.H.C., and Mustapha Mond present the facts of death in the dystopia as well as the social theories behind the practices. Everyone remains young-looking through chemical treatments, until at sixty death comes in the form of "galloping senility," a rapid deterioration of mental and then physical powers. Death is characteristically antiseptic, cheery, and meaningless, underscoring the social belief that the end of any one individual matters very little. The ward in which Linda lies dying in a *soma* trance, then, is strictly conventional by dystopian standards.

But John brings a different consciousness to Linda's death, formed by life and death in Malpais, and Shakespeare's emotional death scenes. Bothered by cheery nurses and curious Delta children, John tries to summon up his childhood memories of his mother, so as to rekindle his love for her and to experience the meaning of his loss. Although the setting distracts John and the children infuriate him, he still has hope of forging a union with his mother that will live beyond her death.

With Linda's whisper, "Popé," however, John realizes that they are still apart, separated by soma and sexual dreaming. To the end, Linda remains the well-conditioned Fordian rather than John's mother. Indeed, her last words are not "my son," or "I love you," but the broken-off hypnopaedic suggestion for recreational sex: "Every one belongs to every . . ."

Style & Language

Note Linda's last look, described in Huxley's phrase as "charged with terror"—the sudden realization of her mortality. To John, the look seems to reproach him; in fact, he believes that he has killed her. John's guilt about his mother's death will re-emerge in later chapters, finally driving him to violence and isolation—an end that Huxley hints at in the conclusion of this chapter, when John pushes away a curious child roughly enough to force him to the floor.

Glossary

caffeine solution Huxley's phrase for a tea-like drink in the brave new world.

Chapter 15

Summary

In the hospital vestibule, John sees Deltas lining up for their *soma* ration. "O brave new world" rings hollowly in his head.

Suddenly inspired, John calls to the Deltas to give up the drug. When they fail to respond, John seizes the *soma* and throws it out the window, causing a riot among the Deltas.

Bernard and Helmholtz arrive to save John, and they become involved in the riot themselves. When the police come, they arrest John as well as Bernard and Helmholtz.

Commentary

This short, but eventful chapter highlights the change in John's perception of the dystopia that will bring about the action propelling the novel toward its conclusion.

Twice earlier, John has quoted the line from Shakespeare's play *The Tempest*, in which Miranda, in awe, contemplates people from the outside world she has never before seen: "O brave new world / That has such people in it!" The first quotation, in Chapter 5, following John's meeting with Bernard and Lenina in Malpais, is straightforward and joyous. The second quotation, in Chapter 8, occurs when John sees several identical Bokanovsky groups working in a factory. Here, John delivers the line ironically, as an expression of his physical disgust at inhuman sameness.

In this chapter, John sees Delta adults lining up for their *soma* ration, and their identical features again appall him. Once more he repeats the quotation, but now the words seems to command him to change the dystopian world into the beautiful ideal he once believed it to be.

In John's sudden inspiration to action, Huxley validates the World State's belief that uncensored literature (the lines from *The Tempest*) and intense emotion—John's sorrow at his mother's death and his disgust at the Delta children in the ward and the Delta adults lined up for *soma*—can result in social unrest. John's surprising call to the Deltas to turn away from *soma* strikes—at least potentially—at the heart of social stability. The Deltas unsurprising fury when John throws the *soma* out the window actually causes a riot, the simplest and most direct form of social instability. Only a *soma* vapor and soothing (anti-revolutionary) words applied immediately can stop the unrest.

Character Insight

Note again, when faced with the confused resistance of the dystopian mind—Lenina's puzzlement at his wooing, the Deltas' resentment at his cries for freedom—John begins with poetry, moves to name-calling, and finally resorts to violence. Frustration and anger boil within John whenever he encounters anyone who does not understand his values and vocabulary.

In this, John is far from a villain, but he is not really a hero, either. Malpais and Shakespeare have sown the seeds of violent fury in him, as well as beauty and tradition. Despite his intentions, John in not the idealistic revolutionary he thinks himself in this chapter.

Note also Helmholtz's enthusiastic participation in the riot, contrasted with Bernard's hesitancy and his attempt to avoid arrest. This contrast—commitment versus cowardice—continues into Chapter 16, when the three men face the judgment of World Controller Mustapha Mond.

Glossary

dolychocephalic having a relatively long head.

bursar a treasurer, as of a college or similar institution. Here, Huxley's term for the person who holds and distributes *soma* at the Park Lane Hospital.

carapace the horny, protective covering over all or part of the back of certain animals, as the upper shell of a turtle, armadillo, crab, etc.

Chapter 16

Summary

In this chapter, John, Bernard, and Helmholtz submit to the judgment of Mustapha Mond. After they discuss the reasons for social control, Mond banishes Bernard and Helmholtz to the Falkland Islands for their role in the riot. Bernard panics, but Helmholtz accepts the new life, far from the pressures of conformity.

Commentary

In this chapter—the aftermath of the *soma* riot—Mustapha Mond discusses the importance of happiness and stability, even at the cost of truth and freedom. In a sense, this is the conversation both John and Helmholtz have been waiting for—the explanation of everything dissatisfying about the supposedly ideal social system.

As a World Controller who makes—and, accordingly, can break—the laws, Mond reveals his own anti-social tendencies. Mond came to an acceptance of dystopian values, he confesses, after a radical youth, during which he experimented with forbidden science. Choosing a position of responsibility in preference to banishment—a decision he regrets at times—Mond explains that he consciously took on the duty of making others happy through social engineering. As someone who controls the dystopian world while remaining aware of its flaws, then, Mond is the perfect character to answer the objections of Helmholtz and John.

In debating with Helmholtz and John, Mond concedes the validity of their literary loyalties. Comparing the feelies and Shakespeare, Mond unhesitatingly comes down on the side of Shakespeare. But he objects to the poetry on social grounds; Shakespeare's tragedies require a dangerous instability, now an outdated concept. Stability, rather than truth or beauty, represents the true human value in this age.

In an extraordinary lecture, Mond defends the society's repressive control over its people—even the development of deliberately brain-damaged fetuses—in the name of human happiness. John's proposal that the predestinators could, at least, make everyone an Alpha meets with an immediate rejection by Mond. The best society, he explains, "is modeled on the iceberg—eight-ninths below the water line, one-ninth above."

Mond's declaration that in his society everyone is happy—even (and, he argues, especially) Epsilons—recalls the image of the Epsilon elevator-operator, sighing in joy at his brief glimpse of the roof before being sent back down into the darkness again. Mond's satisfaction with his own view of the dystopia is apparent, but Huxley leaves the matter of freedom and justice open to the reader.

Note the different ways in which each of the three characters responds to Mond. John seems interested to find someone in the brave new world who can understand (if not share) his values and is even familiar with Shakespeare. John debates Mond directly and intelligently, without lapsing into name-calling or violence as he has with Lenina and later with the Deltas.

For his part, Helmholtz forges a bond of understanding with the World Controller. Both men respect each other, clearly, and Mond even envies Helmholtz his interesting future in banishment, outside the confines of conformity.

In contrast, this chapter reveals Bernard at his lowest point, with all his former daring and rebelliousness evaporated. Silent and anxious throughout the discussion, he panics and breaks down when he hears the sentence of banishment. In Chapter 17, however, Bernard will return, humbled but in better spirits, ready to face his punishment.

Glossary

chary careful or cautious; not given freely.

platitude a commonplace or trite remark.

paroxysm a sudden attack or spasm.

abjection a state of misery and degradation.

scullion a servant doing the rough dirty work in a kitchen. Here, Mustapha Mond uses the word humorously to describe his lowly position early in his career.

Falkland Islands a small group of islands in the South Atlantic Ocean, off the coast of South America. Here, the place of Bernard's and Helmholtz's banishment.

Chapter 17

Summary

In this chapter, Mond and John discuss the brave new world—especially the absence of God. As their discussion unfolds, John expresses his disgust at the casual ease of living in a society where science and conditioning abolish all frustrations. Mond counters that John is claiming "the right" to be unhappy, and John agrees.

John's formal acceptance of all the horrors of sickness, poverty, and fear—capped by Mond's terse "You're welcome"—ends the chapter.

Commentary

In this chapter, Mond continues his discussion of the practical philosophy of the world he controls. With Bernard and Helmholtz gone, Mond and John concentrate on the issues that distinguish the traditional world—John's Malpais as well as the reader's world—from the dystopia, especially a belief in God.

Mond and John's experiences of religion oddly complement one another. Mond knows about God and religion from the forbidden books he has read—the Bible, the medieval *Imitation of Christ*, and the relatively modern works of Cardinal Newman and William James. John, in contrast, has actually lived a religious life in Malpais, surrounded by the rituals of worship and purifying himself in fasting and suffering.

Theme

Mond's argument against religion in his world is materialistic—the main point being that the culture of comfort has made God obsolete. According to Mond's view, people turn to religion only when age and discomfort impel them to look beyond the physical world. But if age and discomfort are banished, the physical, material world never loses its pleasure. Thus, Mond argues, God is irrelevant in the brave new world. In contrast, John's argument stems from a belief in self-denial and suffering as a means to the good—by which he means virtuous—life. Where Mond sees comfort as the pinnacle of human experience, John sees it as a barrier to growth and spirituality. A life of constant amusement and pleasure, he argues, is "degrading."

In his response, Mond accepts the virtues of Christianity—kindness, patience, long-suffering—as reasonable and even socially valuable, but points out that *soma* can do as well as years of painful self-denial in producing virtuous behavior. In a memorable phrase, Mond describes *soma* as "Christianity without tears."

Theme

John, of course, rejects this view immediately, because, according to his definition, a worthwhile human life requires suffering and danger, from which will spring nobility and heroism. The discomfort and the pain, John maintains, are an essential part of freedom, beauty, and religion.

This disclosure brings the discussion—and the novel itself—to its climax. Huxley poses a choice between freedom and comfort. John, the Savage, has made his case for freedom, and Mond for the stability and comfort of the brave new world. The two world-views are obviously incompatible in their own minds, although Huxley leaves open an option for the reader to find a middle way.

Now Mond and John face each other squarely, and the choice emerges clearly. Control means comfort at the loss of freedom. But freedom means the possibility of disease, starvation, and misery. Faced with the choice, John chooses freedom, replying to Mond's list of horrors, after a long silence: "I claim them all."

Style & Language

The obvious misery of freedom's possibilities, John's hesitancy, and Mond's indifference—a noncommittal "You're welcome"—combine to dampen this climactic stand by John. The choice of freedom as it is defined by Mond is not a real victory, and John is still not a true hero.

Both Mond and John show themselves incomplete in this chapter, their different world-views shallow and unimaginative. The conclusion to the discussion will drive John into isolation, but Huxley also means to inspire the reader to explore the assumptions of each character and to think beyond the frame of the novel toward the world itself—and the combinations of freedom and control that might enhance rather than limit life.

Glossary

Cardinal Newman (1801–90) John Henry Newman, English theologian and writer.

neurasthenia a former category of mental disorder, including such symptoms as irritability, fatigue, weakness, anxiety, and localized pains without apparent physical cause, thought to result from weakness or exhaustion of the nervous system. Here, Mustapha Mond's description of normal emotional tension.

Chapter 18

Summary

As Bernard, now calm and resigned, prepares to leave with Helmholtz for the Falklands, John makes plans to retreat to a place of his own, far from the society he has rejected.

In a lighthouse outside London, John undergoes purification for "eating civilization." Fasting, whipping himself, and vomiting, John strives to exorcise the guilt he feels for Linda's death and his horror of sexual contact with Lenina.

Reporters, film crews, and then crowds intrude on his privacy. When Lenina herself approaches him, lovesick and heartbroken, John attacks her with a whip. A riot breaks out and turns into a sexual orgy.

John awakens the next day, groggy from *soma*, and realizes what has happened. Filled with despair and self-loathing, he kills himself.

Commentary

The concluding chapter of the novel brings John the Savage into direct physical conflict with the brave new world he has decided to leave. The sudden violence, shocking as it is, has been prepared for ever since the visit to Malpais and, in some ways, echoes the flagellation ritual Lenina and Bernard witness on the Savage Reservation.

Left on his own, John reveals the true form of his religious feeling—self-destructive rituals of purification by vomiting and whipping himself. Tortured by the memory of his mother's death, he will not let himself enjoy even the simplest pleasures of his austere life—making a bow, for instance.

Theme

The intensity of his self-punishment, the lack of a positive focus for his spiritual feelings, make clear that John's life is not influenced by the hermits of Christianity but by the demons of his own guilt. If the dystopia is the horrifying spectacle of a life with nothing but self-serving comfort, John's lighthouse retreat emerges as the equally horrifying vision of a life with nothing but self-induced pain. As different as they are, both worlds represent emptiness and purposelessness.

In contrast, note Bernard's sudden maturity as he prepares to leave for the Falklands with his fellow-exile, Helmholtz. Their genuine regard for one another and the relative freedom of the island community they are joining give promise of a life much more humane than the one they leave behind.

Outside society, yet still assaulted by the media, just as the suitor of the Maiden of Matsaki is tormented by stinging insects, John suffers a harsher punishment than his friends. In his guilt and isolation, any sexual memories of Lenina immediately incite him to whipping—a penance that draws leering crowds to view him as they would an animal in the zoo.

Character Insight

As a result, John's refuge becomes his cage—his habits of purification a mere trick for the tourists. Free from the trappings of the civilization he hates, John is nevertheless still imprisoned within himself, in his uncontrollable feelings of longing and repulsion. In striving to live a truly human life, John becomes, in the eyes of the crowd, less than human.

Note that John's sexual feelings are still linked to violence, the result of his unintentional conditioning in Malpais. Guilt over his sexual longing for Lenina arouses deep anger that habitually erupts in the ritual flagellation. The original meaning of the whipping—to turn the mind away from thoughts of sexual pleasure—is lost in rage and lust as he imagines whipping Lenina, a disturbing images that looks forward to the end of the chapter.

Literary Device

The "orgy of atonement" represents the sudden, explosive combination of the two worlds of the novel. Overcome by religious and sexual frenzy—a parallel Huxley has already drawn in the Solidarity Service of Chapter 5—John's furious attack on Lenina becomes, in the crowd's conditioned response, "orgy-porgy." Without willing it, John merges into the brave new world he has been trying to escape, yielding to the sexual desire he has so long fought against.

John's suicide represents self-loathing, his disgust at becoming sexually indiscriminate, in the way Linda and Lenina were conditioned to behave. His death puts an end to the possibility of living independently outside the dystopia—except on the socially sanctioned island outposts—or changing it from within.

As he explains in his Foreword to *Brave New World*, Huxley later regretted his decision not to give John a third choice—a middle way between the Savage Reservation and the world of London. *Brave New World Revisited* goes some way in imagining that middle way for the readers of the novel. In this original ending, however, hope for a humane society is lost with the death of its eloquent—if flawed—defender.

Glossary

turpitude   baseness, vileness, depravity. Here used to refer to John's feelings about Lenina.

CHARACTER ANALYSES

Bernard Marx

Bernard Marx receives so much attention in the early part of *Brave New World* that it seems as if Huxley has chosen him for the main character. Later, however, John the Savage takes the central role in the novel.

In a society of perfectly flawless people, Bernard's flaw—his short stature—marks him for ridicule. The rumored cause, alcohol in his blood surrogate, links him chemically to the lower castes and undercuts his Alpha Plus status. Bernard himself is painfully aware of others' responses to his un-Alpha-like shortness, and his lack of confidence stems from anxiety about rejection.

Bernard's feelings about his difference develops into an inner resentment nurtured by his own egotism—a frame of mind that produces much emotion but little action. Although he wants to be an individual, to feel strongly and act freely, Bernard shows little creativity or courage.

Marked as an outsider, Bernard revels in pent-up anger and disgust at those who reject him. To his social equal, Helmholtz, he alternately brags and whines about his anti-social feelings of rebelliousness, yet when faced with superiors, Bernard is characteristically subservient and cowardly. Suddenly a social success, he makes the very most of his association with John to seize the power he once pretended to scorn, flaunting his unorthodoxy just for attention. In this, Bernard proves himself a hypocrite.

When compared with John and Helmholtz, Bernard remains shallow and uninteresting, despite his loneliness and obvious pain. His experience with John and his friendship with Helmholtz, however, bring him to a certain maturity by the end of the novel. Bernard goes to the Falkland Islands more of a real human being than he ever was before.

John the Savage

The only person in the brave new world born naturally of a mother, John represents a unique human being in the novel, with an identity and a family relationship unlike any other character. Although the son of two upper-caste Londoners, he grows up in the squalor of the Savage Reservation. Disconnected, rejected, John is not truly a part of Malpais or of London. His only society is Shakespeare's imaginative world, a realm he inhabits with energy and misguided idealism.

John is the true loner, the individual Bernard imagines himself at times, and his life, accordingly, is filled with confusion and pain.

John represents the most important and most complex character of *Brave New World*, a stark contrast to Bernard, the would-be rebel. Bernard's dissatisfaction with his society expresses itself most characteristically in sullen resentment and imagined heroism, but John lives out his ideals, however unwisely. In turning aside Lenina's advances, John rejects the society's values. He acts boldly in calling the Deltas to rebellion and in throwing out the soma. Finally, he faces the powerful Mustapha Mond deliberately and intelligently and sets out on his own to create a life for himself, which ends in tragedy.

If anyone, John should be the character to challenge and to bring down the Brave New World that is stifling humanity. In the end, John cannot change the society, because he is blocked within and without. Mustapha Mond makes clear the power of the World State to resist any unstablizing force. But John is also held back by his own destructive tendencies toward violence and self-loathing.

Although John despises conditioning, Huxley reveals that John has been conditioned, too. Because of the terrible conditions of his life in Malpais, John associates sex with humiliation and pain and character with suffering, and this destructive view gains further power in John's response to the poetry of Shakespeare.

John's conditioning limits his ability to act freely, making him a deeply flawed potential hero. His death is the result of his own imperfect understanding as well as the inhuman forces of the brave new world.

Lenina

"Awfully pneumatic" and proud of her sexual attractiveness, Lenina seems at first a conventional woman of a society in which comfort, pleasure, and materialism are the only values. As the novel progresses, however, Lenina emerges as a conflicted character, more complex than she seems initially.

Although she may not acknowledge it, Lenina rebels against her conditioning for sexual promiscuity, the belief that "every one belongs to every one else." At the onset, she is continuing an unconventionally long and exclusive sexual relationship with Henry Foster. Even in returning to normal sexual behavior, she again rebels, choosing the socially misfit Bernard Marx. Without completely understanding her motivations, Lenina explores the emotional territory outside recreational sex with far more daring than Bernard, the supposed rebel.

Lenina's relationship with John brings her to an emotional, physical, but not intellectual experience of love, while her unaccustomed vulnerability makes her the victim of John's violence twice. She represents the rare potential to see beyond conditioning, but cannot live freely.

Linda

A thoroughly conventional brave new world women dropped unexpectedly in a very different society, Linda faces the challenge of understanding traditional morality. But Linda's sense of the normal moral world—drilled into her by her early conditioning—consists of equal parts recreational sex and soothing drugs. Beyond finding the rough equivalents of her own world's social occupations—peyote and mescal for *soma*, for instance—she never seriously engages the culture she lives in. As a result, she remains isolated, condemning her son John to a marginal existence as well.

As Linda herself points out, she has no training for the life she has had to live as a mother. Filled with shame for having a baby and longing for her home, Linda wraps herself in a blanket of mescal and peyote, remaining intoxicated and barely aware of John and his needs as a growing young man. For John, she feels an intense mixture of love and revulsion, complicated further by her obsession with Popé. The strange quality of his mother's feelings for him obviously has an effect on John himself, especially in his relationships with women.

After her long years of struggle and shame on the Savage Reservation, Linda throws herself into *soma* holidays, shortening her life by her addiction. At the end, for the confused, angry woman, death comes as a release, despite her terror.

The D.H.C.

The Director of Hatcheries and Conditioning—or "Tomakin," as Linda calls him—seems at first a strictly conventional man, absolutely conservative in his outlook and demeanor. Respectful to superiors, snappish—even cruel—with anti-social inferiors like Bernard, he upholds the highest standards of brave new world morality.

Yet, paradoxically, he has had an intense experience of love and regret that has changed him inwardly forever. His sadness at losing Linda and the guilt he feels for leaving her represent truly human responses in an inhuman world. Sensibly, the D.H.C. keeps the memory of Linda to himself for all the years he climbs the career ladder. The unexpected reminder of the Savage Reservation catches him off guard, leaving him vulnerable, first to fear of exposure and then to Bernard's plan for revenge.

With the D.H.C., Huxley emphasizes the connection of fear of discovery with hypocrisy. Bernard's exposure of the D.H.C.'s relationship with Linda and John, their son, gains most of its energy and comic force from the D.H.C.'s hypocritical denunciation of anti-social behavior. In this, the character and his public humiliation recall traditional unmasking scenes in fiction involving corrupt religious or other well-respected social figures. Still, the D.H.C. shows himself very human in the long-term emotional effects of his traumatic situation. Again, Huxley hints at the possibility of true feelings despite conditioning but undercuts the hope in the end.

Mustapha Mond

The Controller, one of the ten men who run the World State, represents a combination of past and present, convention and rebellion. A man of two worlds, Mond is familiar with the history that others are forbidden to know, and so his thinking ranges both inside and outside the present social order. The maker of the rules, as he says, can break them as well, if he wishes.

Only Mond's extraordinary power keeps him safe from whispers of his dangerous knowledge and collection of unorthodox books. He is untouchable but not unreachable. With Helmholtz and John, Mond discusses the unspoken assumptions of the society they find so constricting, even confessing his own youthful experiments in challenging authority. Mond knows the nature of the malcontent—he once was one—but he is committed to keeping the society stable. He uses his power for others' happiness, he explains, not his own.

During his lectures, Mond expresses his unique views on the themes of freedom, happiness, civilization, and heroism. His dry delivery contributes much to the satiric tone of the novel. In his intellect and wit, Mond is the character who most resembles Huxley himself.

Helmholtz Watson

Helmholtz represents a sharp contrast to his close friend, Bernard. Unlike the flighty, whiny Bernard, Helmholtz shows himself to be emotionally stable even in his deep dissatisfaction. Bored with mindless recreational sex and *soma*-taking, he simply abstains, saving his energies for what he believes to be more valuable activity. In this, Helmholtz shows himself to be a more serious rebel than Bernard.

Helmholtz voices the inarticulate feeling of meaningless in the life of brave new world citizens. Helmholtz has something to say, he believes, but he cannot find the words within him. In his struggle to find meaning and expression for his feeling of emptiness, Helmholtz emerges as one of the most fully human and engaging characters of the novel.

CRITICAL ESSAYS

Society and the Individual
in *Brave New World*

"Every one belongs to every one else," whispers the voice in the dreams of the young in Huxley's future world—the hypnopaedic suggestion discouraging exclusivity in friendship and love. In a sense in this world, every one *is* every one else as well. All the fetal conditioning, hypnopaedic training, and the power of convention molds each individual into an inter-changeable part in the society, valuable only for the purpose of making the whole run smoothly. In such a world, uniqueness is uselessness and uniformity is bliss, because social stability is everything.

In the first chapter, the D.H.C. proudly explains the biochemical technology that makes possible the production of virtually identical human beings and, in doing so, introduces Huxley's theme of individ-uality under assault. Bokanovsky's Process, which arrests normal human development while promoting the production of dozens of identical eggs, deliberately deprives human beings of their unique, individual natures and so makes overt processes for controlling them unnecessary.

The uniformity of the Gammas, Deltas, and Epsilons is accom-plished by careful poisoning with alcohol and produces—in Huxley's word—"sub-human" people, capable of work but not of independent thought. For these lower-caste men and women, individuality is liter-ally impossible. As a result, built on a large foundation of identical, eas-ily manipulated people, the society thrives. Stability lives, but individuality—the desire and/or ability to be different—is dead.

"When the individual feels, society reels," Lenina piously reminds Bernard, who strives without success for a genuine human emotion beyond his customary peevishness. This inability is a kind of tragic flaw in Bernard. Even love—acknowledging and cherishing another's unique identity—represents a threat to stability founded on uniformity. The dystopia's alternative—recreational sex—is deliberately designed to blur the distinctions among lovers and between emotions and urges, find-ing its social and ritual expression in "Orgy-Porgy."

This organized release of sexual urges undercuts passion, the intense feeling of one person for another, as the individuals subordinate even their own sexual pleasure to the supposed joy of their society's unity. At the Solidarity Service, Bernard finds the exercise degrading, just as any-one clinging to any idealism about sex would be revolted. John's sensi-tive feelings about love suffer even from the representation of such an orgy at the feelies. Significantly, it is the morning after his own experience of "orgy-porgy" that John commits suicide. His most private, cherished sense of love and of self, he feels, has been violated.

In Huxley's dystopia, the drug *soma* also serves to keep individuals from experiencing the stressful negative affects of conflicts that the society cannot prevent. Pain and stress—grief, humiliation, disappointment—representing uniquely individual reactions to conflict still occur sometimes in the brave new world. The people of the brave new world "solve" their conflict problems by swallowing a few tablets or taking an extended *soma*-holiday, which removes or sufficiently masks the negative feelings and emotions that other, more creative, problem-solving techniques might have and which cuts off the possibility of action that might have socially disruptive or revolutionary results.

The society, therefore, encourages everyone to take *soma* as a means of social control by eliminating the affects of conflict. John's plea to the Deltas to throw away their *soma*, then, constitutes a cry for rebellion that goes unheeded. *Soma*-tized people do not know their own degradation. They are not even fully conscious that they are individuals.

Both Bernard and John struggle against the society's constant efforts to undermine their individuality, but one character reveals a deeper understanding of the stakes than the other. Bernard rails loudly about the inhumanity of the system. His outrage stems from the injustices he suffers personally, but he apparently is unwilling or unable to fathom a debate or course of action against the malady because he is an Alpha Plus upon whom the process has been at least partially successful. Once Bernard receives the sexual and social attention he believes is his due, his complaints continue merely as a show of daring and bravado. He sees no reason and feels no moral or social compunction to fight for the rights of others oppressed by the social system.

John, on the other hand, truly challenges the brave new world with a view of freedom that includes everyone, even the Deltas who reject his call for rebellion. Although John, like Bernard, suffers from the oppression of the World State, John is able to frame his objections philosophically and debate the issue face to face with World Controller Mustapha Mond because, although John is genetically an Alpha Plus, he has not undergone the conditioning necessary to conform. His objection is not only his own lack of comfort, but the degradation of slavery imposed by the society. John's acceptance of a free human life with all its danger and pain represents an idealistic stand beyond Bernard's comprehension or courage. Flawed, misguided, John nevertheless dares to claim his right to be an individual.

By the end of the novel, all the efforts to free the individual from the grip of the World State have failed, destroyed by the power of convention induced by hypnopaedia and mob psychology. Only Helmholtz and Bernard, bound for banishment in the Falkland Islands, represent the possibility of a slight hope—a limited freedom within the confines of a restrictive society.

The battle for individuality and freedom ends with defeat in *Brave New World*—a decision Huxley later came to regret. In *Brave New World Revisited*, a series of essays on topics suggested by the novel, Huxley emphasizes the necessity of resisting the power of tyranny by keeping one's mind active and free. The individual freedoms may be limited in the modern world, Huxley admits, but they must be exercised constantly or be lost.

Brave New World Revisited: Further Thoughts on the Future

In 1958, Aldous Huxley published a collection of essays on the same social, political, and economic themes he had explored earlier in his novel *Brave New World*. Although the form differs—the work is nonfiction instead of fiction—Huxley's characteristic intelligence and wit enlivens the essays of *Brave New World Revisited* just as it did in his novel.

Brave New World has been called a "novel of ideas," because Huxley takes as his primary focus for the fiction the contrast and clash of different assumptions and theories rather than merely the conflict of personalities. In *Brave New World Revisited*, Huxley dispenses with the fictional construct altogether and lets the ideas themselves form and inform his work. In a sense, then, Huxley opened his debate about the future in fiction—for artistic purposes—and then continued it in philosophy with persuasion in mind.

Part of Huxley's reason for "revisiting" the themes of *Brave New World* stems from his horrified recognition that the world he created in fiction was in fact becoming a reality. In the depths of the Cold War, a totalitarian world state—a Communist dictatorship, perhaps—seemed a distinct possibility; and so, with the world on the verge of destruction or tyranny, Huxley felt compelled to search for and find the hope for freedom missing in his novel.

In describing the modern, postwar world, Huxley acknowledges the prophetic power of George Orwell's *1984*. In communist nations, Huxley points out, leaders used to control individuals with punishment, just as the representatives of Big Brother frighten and at times torture citizens into submission in Orwell's novel. But in the Soviet Union at least, the death of Stalin brought an end to the "old-fashioned" form of universal tyranny. By the late 1950s, in the Soviet bloc, governments attempted to control high-ranking individuals with rewards—just as in *Brave New World*. Meanwhile, the government continued to enforce conformity on the masses by fear of punishment. Communist totalitarianism, therefore, combined the *Brave New World* and *1984* styles of oppression. Both novels proved sadly prophetic.

Still, Huxley argues, the future will look more like *Brave New World* than *1984*. In the West, pleasure and distraction, used by those in power, control people's spending, political loyalties, and even their thoughts. Control through reward poses a greater threat to human freedom because, unlike punishment, it can be introduced unconsciously and continued indefinitely, with the approval and support of the people being controlled.

In place of the Nine Years' War—the calamity that brought the society of *Brave New World* into being—Huxley points to the danger of overpopulation as the trigger for tyranny. Just as the fictional war brought the call for a totalitarian World State, the chaos caused by overpopulation may be demanding control through over organization. Instead of many little businesses producing necessities, an over-organized society allows big business to mass-produce anything and everything saleable, while controlling consumer spending through commercials and social pressure. The resulting programmed consumption— "Ending is better than mending"—of *Brave New World* had already begun to take over the post-war world, at least in the West.

The literal consumption of *soma*-like drugs also captures Huxley's attention. By the 1950s, readily available tranquilizers adjusted people to a maladjusted culture, smoothing out any inconvenient instincts of resistance, just as a *soma*-holiday eliminated the recognition of unhappiness.

Huxley takes particular pride, mixed with dismay, at the prophetic quality of his own future vision. In the 1950s, commercial jingles—

what Huxley calls "singing commercials"—seem to invade and take over the conscious mind and culture, in the same way that the brave new world runs smoothly on the slogans of hypnopaedia. Hypnopaedia itself, of course, was a well-respected reality by the time of *Brave New World Revisited.* And the use of subliminal persuasion, a method for introducing subconscious suggestions, had already caused a scandal in American movies. Although subliminal persuasion does not appear in *Brave New World,* Huxley wishes aloud that he had included it, since the unconscious power of the suggestions seems perfect for the cheery authoritarianism of the dystopia.

In general, Huxley warns his readers that they may be talking themselves into accepting a world that they would reject, if only they were fully conscious of its nature. But, distracted by consumerism and pleasure, people seldom truly engage the reality they are living, just as the citizens of the brave new world seldom recognize the restraints of their society. Unconscious manipulation through language—propaganda—keeps individual minds open to any suggestions, even the most inhuman.

Huxley cites, from recent history, Hitler's power of manipulation through language as a frightening example. Quoting from the dictator's autobiography, Huxley emphasizes the importance of Hitler's skillful use of propaganda in motivating citizens to support his leadership. Hitler, for instance, deliberately scheduled his public addresses at night, a time when fatigue makes people vulnerable to suggestion, excitable, and most likely to succumb to the mass hysteria Hitler produced at his rallies. Huxley's fictional Controllers of the brave new world follow the same pattern with the Solidarity Services, a ritual of programmed mass hysteria to produce social loyalty. A different form of the same suggestibility occurs in light sleep, the period when the hypnopaedic voices whisper society's wisdom into the ears of children and young adults. In both cases, the rational self has its guards down, and any message—however irrational—may make its way into the mind and influence behavior.

According to Huxley, even in the 1950s, propaganda emanates from those who want to control behavior on a large scale, just as the World Controllers of *Brave New World* want to maintain stability. Dictators like Hitler use propaganda to whip up support and to direct violence against anyone identified as the enemy. In the 1950s, Huxley argues, propaganda represents the principal tool of the "Power Elite," C. Wright Mills' term for the government and business leaders controlling communication and the economy. Through commercials, subliminal messages, and careful suppression of challenging truths, Huxley declares, propaganda is infiltrating the language of society, becoming perhaps the only way to speak at all. If the trend continues, Westerners may be in danger of becoming as unconsciously manipulated and enslaved as the citizens of the brave new world.

Identifying the enemy of freedom as propaganda, Huxley finds the solution that eluded him in *Brave New World*. Education in the recognition and resistance of propaganda must be the responsibility of every individual. Referring to the brief history of the Institute for Propaganda Analysis, Huxley emphasizes that government and other authorities may oppose the unmasking of anti-rational, manipulative language for their own reasons. Still, Huxley insists, the only hope lies in the active mind, able and willing to make its own judgments. Individual freedom, compassion, and intelligence—the very qualities missing in the dystopia of *Brave New World*—can guide the fully conscious, fully human mind into a truly free, truly human future.

CliffsNotes Review

Use this CliffsNotes Review to test your understanding of the original text and reinforce what you've learned in this book. After you work through the review and essay questions, identify the quote section, and the fun and useful practice projects, you're well on your way to understanding a comprehensive and meaningful interpretation of *Brave New World*.

Q&A

1. Early in the novel, Fanny Crowne lectures Lenina for her unacceptable social behavior. What is Lenina's fault, as Fanny sees it?

   a. Lenina is "too pneumatic"

   b. Lenina is not promiscuous enough

   c. Lenina is consuming too much soma

2. What do people believe to be the cause of Bernard's strange character?

   a. a serious fall in infancy

   b. a difficult adolescence

   c. alcohol in his blood surrogate

3. Mustapha Mond is one of the ten World Controllers. What is his position on forbidden books?

   a. he owns many of them himself

   b. he enjoys reading them in secret

   c. he believes they must be suppressed

4. John is born and grows up in Malpais, but he cannot join in the initiation rite that marks the beginning of manhood. Why do the elders reject him?

   a. John has failed a crucial test

   b. John's mother is sexually active with more than one man

   c. John has no father

5. Which brave new world drug does Mustapha Mond describe as "Christianity without tears"?

   a. sex-hormone chewing gum

   b. *soma*

   c. violent passion surrogate

   Answers: (1) b. (2) c. (3) a, b, and c. (4) b. (5) b.

Identify the Quote

1. Community. Identity. Stability.

2. I'm thinking of a queer feeling I sometimes get, a feeling that I've got something important to say and the power to say it—only I don't know what it is, and I can't make any use of the power.

3. Don't you want to be free and men? Don't you even understand what manhood and freedom are?

4. Christianity without tears—that's what *soma* is.

5. Perhaps the forces that now menace freedom are too strong to be resisted for very long. It is still our duty to do whatever we can to resist them.

Answers: (1) The motto of the World State, displayed on the shield of the Central London Hatchery and Conditioning Centre, repeated by the D.H.C. in his address to the students. (2) Helmholtz Watson to Bernard Marx, on the frustrations of writing anything meaningful in the dystopia. (3) John calling out to a crowd of Deltas to throw away their *soma*. (4) World Controller Mustapha Mond, explaining the benefits of *soma* to John. (5) Huxley on the challenge of the future in *Brave New World Revisited*.

Essay Questions

1. Although they were raised very differently, Bernard Marx and John the Savage are both dissatisfied with the society of the brave new world. What qualities do the characters have in common? How are they different? Compare their strengths and weaknesses.

2. In some ways, Linda and Lenina are the most serious rebels of the brave new world. How does the experience of each character challenge the assumptions of the dystopia? Do you think Huxley takes these women characters as seriously as he does the men? Why or why not?

3. In *Brave New World Revisited*, Huxley discusses the modern world's resemblance to his dystopia. Make your own case for or against his prophecies. Is modern life really a version of the brave new world? Be specific in your answer, referring to social, political, and economic trends. If modern life is a brave new world, what solutions can you offer?

4. Analyze Mustapha Mond's role in the novel. How is the World Controller different from the other characters? What is Huxley's purpose is putting Mond in *Brave New World*? What would the novel be like without Mond?

5. Discuss Huxley's use of satire to make his point in the novel. Choose either the scene describing the Solidarity Service that Bernard attends or John's visit to the feelies as the focus for your argument.

6. Henry Ford, inventor of the assembly line that made possible mass production, looms large as a kind of god in the brave new world. Discuss the specific ways that the society uses Ford's methods to maintain stability. How does Huxley use Ford and the assembly line to advance his themes?

7. "Everybody's happy nowadays," according to the hypnopaedic suggestion. Mustapha Mond himself asserts that happiness and stability are the hallmarks of his society. What evidence does Huxley offer that this is not true? In what specific ways has the promise of happiness not been achieved in the brave new world?

Practice Projects

1. Write a short sequel to *Brave New World*, exploring the life of Helmholtz and Bernard on the Falkland Islands. What kind of world do the banished men find? Is it truly free, or just another kind of conformity? Is one character more adaptable than the other? Create your sequel as a short story or a play.

2. The confrontation between Mond and John—the heart of the novel—represents a conversation between two diametrically opposed characters. Dramatize the discussion as a play for performance by crafting Huxley's prose into believable dialogue as well as creating set design and costuming to support the future setting.

3. Many contemporary movies have drawn on *Brave New World* for inspiration in imagining a future world. Compile a filmography of those movies you believe draw on themes or atmosphere first presented in Huxley's novel and explain why you have chosen them. (Possibilities might include *Blade Runner* and *2001: A Space Odyssey*.)

4. Taking the view of either an architect or set designer, imagine and design your own sketches or models of Huxley's world.

5. In Huxley's new introduction to his novel, he expresses regret that he did not imagine a "middle way" for John the Savage, between the "lunacy" of the Savage Reservation and the "insanity" of London. Sketch out a scenario in which you imagine another possibility for John's life after leaving London that would create a more hopeful ending for the novel.

CliffsNotes Resource Center

The learning doesn't need to stop here. CliffsNotes Resource Center shows you the best of the best—links to the best information in print and online about the author and/or related works. And don't think that this is all we've prepared for you; we've put all kinds of pertinent information at www.cliffsnotes.com. Look for all the terrific resources at your favorite bookstore or local library and on the Internet. When you're online, make your first stop www.cliffsnotes.com where you'll find more incredibly useful information about *Brave New World*.

Books

This CliffsNotes book provides a meaningful interpretation of Brave New World, published by IDG Books Worldwide, Inc. If you are looking for information about the author and/or related works, check out these other publications:

Aldous Huxley: A Study of the Major Novels, by Peter Bowering. A thorough critical analysis of Huxley's major fictional works, with chapters on the novel of ideas and *Brave New World.* The work considers Huxley both as a moralist and an artist, as reflected in the themes in his novels of ideas. New York: Oxford University Press, 1969.

A Clockwork Orange, by Anthony Burgess. A novel set in a future where behavior is controlled through chemical conditioning. The work combines elements of *Brave New World* and *1984* with a contemporary concern for violent crime by teenagers. New York: Ballantine, 1962.

Aldous Huxley Recollected: An Oral History, by David King Dunaway. A biographical portrait of Huxley drawn from the reminiscences of his family, friends, and colleagues. The book focuses primarily on Huxley's later life in California after World War II. New York: Carroll and Graf Publishers, 1995.

Aldous Huxley: Satirist and Novelist, by Peter Firchow. This study includes a chapter on *Brave New World* and Huxley's later utopian novel, *Ape and Essence.* Firchow argues that *Brave New World* represents a satire not of the future (a pointless exercise, in the critic's view) but of the present. Firchow also sees the germ for *Brave New*

World in Huxley's first novel, *Crome Yellow*, in the character's Scogan's plan for a "Rational State." Minneapolis: University of Minnesota Press, 1972.

Between the Wars: Essays and Letters, by Aldous Huxley, edited by David Bradshaw. This collection of nonfiction writing dates from the period when Huxley was writing *Brave New World*. It includes essays such as "Science and Civilization" (1932), "What is Happening to Our Population?" (1934), "Babies—State Property" (1930), and "How to Improve the World" (1936). Chicago: Ivan R. Dee, 1994.

Critical Essays on Aldous Huxley. Jerome Meckier, ed. This collection features a fine introduction focusing on the "novel of ideas." Essays on Huxley's major novels include "The Manuscript Revisions of *Brave New World*," "*Brave New World* and the Rationalization of Industry," and "Technology and Gender in Aldous Huxley's Alternative Worlds." New York: G.K. Hall and Company, 1996.

1984, by George Orwell. Orwell's dark vision of a future London, influenced by the Huxley's *Brave New World* and Orwell's own experience of the dreary foreboding of postwar Britain. Big Brother's image represents the conditioning power of the dystopia—a visual form of hypnopaedia—while O'Brien, who explains the society to the main character, serves as a kind of Mustapha Mond in the novel. New York: Penguin, 1984.

Aldous Huxley: The Critical Heritage. Donald Watt, ed. This collection offers contemporary reviews of *Brave New World*. Critics responding to the novel at the time it was published include philosopher Bertrand Russell and novelist Hermann Hesse. Boston: Routledge and Kegan Paul, 1975.

Aldous Huxley, by Harold H Watts. The study features a chapter on *Brave New World* and the essay "The Mind of Aldous Huxley." The book also includes a very useful biography and chronology. Boston: Twayne Publishers, 1969.

It's easy to find books published by IDG Books Worldwide, Inc. You'll find them in your favorite bookstores (on the Internet and at a store near you). We also have three Web sites that you can use to read about all the books we publish:

- www.cliffsnotes.com
- www.dummies.com
- www.idgbooks.com

Internet

Check out these Web resources for more information about Aldous Huxley and *Brave New World*:

Aldous Huxley Soma Web, `http://www.primenet.com/~matthew/huxley`—The site includes texts, photos, and articles about Huxley's *Brave New World*. There are also links to other sites featuring films based on the novel as well as television dramas, like "Gattica," that offer a vision of a similar future.

The Island Web, `http://www.island.org/Huxley`—The site offers excerpts from Huxley's last novel. It also includes Huxley's thoughts on the future, humanity, and mysticism, as well as poetry taken from the pages of "Island."

Shadows of an Invisible Man: The Role of Individuality in Invisible Man and Brave New World. `http://www.oakland.edu/~jcoughli/distopia.htm`—This site offers an insightful comparison of Huxley's novel with author Ralph Ellison's *Invisible Man*. The featured essay compares the challenges of the dystopia of *Brave New World* and the real world of racism.

Next time you're on the Internet, don't forget to drop by `www.cliffsnotes.com`. We created an online Resource Center that you can use today, tomorrow, and beyond.

Films and Other Recordings

Brave New World. Dir. Leslie Libman and Larry Williams. Perf: Peter Gallagher, Leonard Nimoy, Miguel Ferrer. NBC. 3 May 1998. This television movie features Nimoy as Mustapha Mond in an orange Nehru jacket and concentrates on the representation of Huxley's futuristic conditioning. Depicting the training of the various castes, for example, the film features the kind of quick-cuts now common in video. The future, the film seems to be saying, is now.

"Huxley and Cloning." *Morning Edition.* Natl. Public Radio. 12 Aug. 1997. In this radio broadcast, Huxley biographer David Dunaway takes another look at *Brave New World* in light of the recent developments in genetic engineering.

Brave New World. CBS Radio Workshop. CBS Radio. 27 Jan. 1956 and 3 Feb. 1956. Originally broadcast on radio in an unconventional anthology series, these recordings feature Aldous Huxley narrating an hour-long adaption of his novel. Available in RealAudio at Seeing Eye Theater at http://www.scifi.com/set/classics/brave.

Send Us Your Favorite Tips

In your quest for knowledge, have you ever experienced that sublime moment when you figure out a trick that saves time or trouble? Perhaps you realized you were taking ten steps to accomplish something that could have taken two. Or you found a little-known workaround that achieved great results. If you've discovered a useful tip that gave you insight into or helped you understand *Brave New World* and you'd like to share it, the CliffsNotes staff would love to hear from you. Go to our Web site at www.cliffsnotes.com and click the Talk to Us button. If we select your tip, we may publish it as part of CliffsNotes Daily, our exciting, free e-mail newsletter. To find out more or to subscribe to a newsletter, go to www.cliffsnotes.com on the Web.

Index

NOTES

NOTES

NOTES

NOTES

liffsNotes

ITERATURE
OTES

osalom, Absalom!
he Aeneid
gamemnon
ice in Wonderland
l the King's Men
l the Pretty Horses
l Quiet on the
  Western Front
l's Well &
  Merry Wives
nerican Poets of the
  20th Century
nerican Tragedy
himal Farm
na Karenina
them
ntony and Cleopatra
istotle's Ethics
l Lay Dying
e Assistant
You Like It
las Shrugged
tobiography of
  Ben Franklin
tobiography of
  Malcolm X
e Awakening
bbit
rtleby & Benito
  Cereno
e Bean Trees
e Bear
e Bell Jar
oved
wulf
e Bible
y Budd & Typee
ck Boy
ck Like Me
ak House
ss Me, Ultima
e Bluest Eye & Sula
ve New World
thers Karamazov

The Call of the Wild &
  White Fang
Candide
The Canterbury Tales
Catch-22
Catcher in the Rye
The Chosen
The Color Purple
Comedy of Errors…
Connecticut Yankee
The Contender
The Count of
  Monte Cristo
Crime and Punishment
The Crucible
Cry, the Beloved
  Country
Cyrano de Bergerac
Daisy Miller &
  Turn…Screw
David Copperfield
Death of a Salesman
The Deerslayer
Diary of Anne Frank
Divine Comedy-I.
  Inferno
Divine Comedy-II.
  Purgatorio
Divine Comedy-III.
  Paradiso
Doctor Faustus
Dr. Jekyll and Mr. Hyde
Don Juan
Don Quixote
Dracula
Electra & Medea
Emerson's Essays
Emily Dickinson Poems
Emma
Ethan Frome
The Faerie Queene
Fahrenheit 451
Far from the Madding
  Crowd
A Farewell to Arms
Farewell to Manzanar
Fathers and Sons
Faulkner's Short Stories

Faust Pt. I & Pt. II
The Federalist
Flowers for Algernon
For Whom the Bell Tolls
The Fountainhead
Frankenstein
The French
  Lieutenant's Woman
The Giver
Glass Menagerie &
  Streetcar
Go Down, Moses
The Good Earth
The Grapes of Wrath
Great Expectations
The Great Gatsby
Greek Classics
Gulliver's Travels
Hamlet
The Handmaid's Tale
Hard Times
Heart of Darkness &
  Secret Sharer
Hemingway's
  Short Stories
Henry IV Part 1
Henry IV Part 2
Henry V
House Made of Dawn
The House of the
  Seven Gables
Huckleberry Finn
I Know Why the
  Caged Bird Sings
Ibsen's Plays I
Ibsen's Plays II
The Idiot
Idylls of the King
The Iliad
Incidents in the Life of
  a Slave Girl
Inherit the Wind
Invisible Man
Ivanhoe
Jane Eyre
Joseph Andrews
The Joy Luck Club
Jude the Obscure

Julius Caesar
The Jungle
Kafka's Short Stories
Keats & Shelley
The Killer Angels
King Lear
The Kitchen God's Wife
The Last of the
  Mohicans
Le Morte d'Arthur
Leaves of Grass
Les Miserables
A Lesson Before Dying
Light in August
The Light in the Forest
Lord Jim
Lord of the Flies
The Lord of the Rings
Lost Horizon
Lysistrata & Other
  Comedies
Macbeth
Madame Bovary
Main Street
The Mayor of
  Casterbridge
Measure for Measure
The Merchant
  of Venice
Middlemarch
A Midsummer Night's
  Dream
The Mill on the Floss
Moby-Dick
Moll Flanders
Mrs. Dalloway
Much Ado About
  Nothing
My Ántonia
Mythology
Narr. …Frederick
  Douglass
Native Son
New Testament
Night
1984
Notes from the
  Underground

Check Out the All-New CliffsNotes Guides

TECHNOLOGY TOPICS

PERSONAL FINANCE TOPICS

CAREER TOPICS